D1137905

God's story in
60 snapshots

bible[60]

Andy Peck

CWR

Copyright © CWR 2013

Published and reprinted 2013 by CWR, Waverley Abbey House, Waverley Lane, Farnham, Surrey GU9 8EP, UK. CWR is a Registered Charity – Number 294387 and a Limited Company registered in England – Registration Number 1990308.

The right of Andy Peck to be identified as the author of this work has been asserted by him in accordance with the Copyright, Designs and Patents Act 1988, sections 77 and 78.

All rights reserved. No part of this publication may be reproduced, stored in a retrieval system or transmitted, in any form or by any means, electronic, mechanical, photocopying, recording or otherwise, without the prior permission in writing of CWR.

See back of book for list of National Distributors.

Unless otherwise indicated, all Scripture references are from The Holy Bible, New International Version (Anglicised edition), copyright © 1979, 1984, 2011 by Biblica (formerly the International Bible Society).

Concept development, editing, design and production by CWR

Printed in the United Kingdom by Page Bros, Norwich

ISBN: 978-1-85345-923-8

Contents

Acknowledgments

My particular thanks to Lynette Brooks, Director of Publishing at CWR, who suggested the idea of this book and gave me the idea for a sixty-day format. It was a joy to write, not least as it provided a regular focus on God and His Word at a tough time in the life of our family, and for me personally.

I want to acknowledge books that helped me particularly: *A Light to the Nations: The Missional Church and the Biblical Story* by Michael W. Goheen (Grand Rapids, MI: Baker Academic, 2011) and *The Wrong Messiah: The Real Story of Jesus of Nazareth* by Nick Page (London: Hodder & Stoughton, 2011). The latter was a particular blessing in preparing to lead a trip to Israel in 2011, and in understanding the Gospel narratives.

I have benefited much from my friend and colleague Phil Greenslade's understanding of the Bible's narrative. His work on 'God's story' reflected in his book *A Passion for God's Story* (Carlisle: Paternoster Press, 2002), and courses by that name at CWR have led many into a fuller understanding of what the Bible is really about. I am grateful for Phil's many insights that have refreshed and challenged my perspectives, and commend his courses to you – visit www.cwr.org.uk/training for further details.

Introduction

You are pressed for time and realise that your listener is struggling to stay interested. So you might say, 'To cut a long story short ...' and provide a summary of the main points you want to make. There is always more that could be told of any story, but isolating the major points is a vital skill, especially if you want to keep your friends.

This book aims to cut the long story of the Bible into a shorter one. It looks at the key turning points and parts of the narrative that are critical for a grasp of the story that God is telling in the Bible.

It is my hope that an understanding of the major turning points will compel you to return to the books of the Bible at another time, keen to more easily enjoy their treasure once the overall thrust of Scripture is understood. So the readings in this book must not be seen as a substitute for reading the whole of the books. I am keenly aware of the danger of taking texts out of their overall context. My aim is that the notes accompanying the reading of the Bible passages show how the selected chapter or section fits into the overall story.

My selection of passages is made largely with the narrative of Scripture in mind. In places I have chosen passages according to their believed chronological order, rather than their order in a typical Bible. I have included some sections that demonstrate the book that they are part of, even if narrative was not moved forward by them. It would have seemed odd, for example, not to have included something from Psalms and Proverbs. As such, some important major themes of Scripture are covered along the way, but not in detail. Themes such as the character of God, redemption, sacrifice or the kingdom of God, could all be usefully followed up in more detail than is possible here.

'JESUS CENTRAL'

I have chosen thirty readings from the Old Testament part of the Bible and thirty from the New, even though the Old has far more books and covers a longer period of biblical history. The Old Testament covers over 2,000 years compared to the less than 100 years in the New, but I opted for this ratio because of the centrality of an understanding of Jesus in the New Testament to grasping what the Bible is about. Scripture sees the coming of 'God, the Son', Jesus Christ, to earth as central to an understanding. Jesus Himself said to the religious leaders of His day, 'You diligently study the Scriptures because you think that by them you possess eternal life. These are the Scriptures that testify about me, yet you refuse to come to me to have life' (John 5:39–40).

After His resurrection, Jesus spoke to two of His disciples as they travelled to Emmaus, a town near Jerusalem. Not recognising Him, the disciples were despondent because they thought Jesus was still dead. Jesus said to them, '"Did not the Christ have to suffer these things and then enter his glory?" And beginning with Moses and all the Prophets, he explained to them what was said in all the Scriptures concerning himself' (Luke 24:26–27).

Later the apostle Paul would write, 'For no matter how many promises God has made, they are "Yes" in Christ. And so through him the "Amen" is spoken by us to the glory of God' (2 Corinthians 1:20).

God had determined to bless the world and reverse the curse of sin pronounced in the Garden of Eden. He chose to do so by His election of a people who would be the model community showing the world what He is like. But their failure to display His goodness is a permanent reminder to us of human failure and the need for One to come who was fully man and fully God, to deal finally with the problem of human sin and realise the potential that image bearers can have as they relate to their Maker.

God's dealings with humans in the Old Testament were always preliminary to the coming of Jesus in the New Testament. In the light of the events of the New, chiefly the life, death and resurrection of Jesus, we can make sense of what God was doing.

Jesus, through a new agreement with humankind (known as the new covenant), promises the wonderful blessing of His Holy Spirit, who comes to live in His followers, empowering them to live each day with Him at the heart of their lives.

Hence the Bible is written not to you but *for you*. As the apostle Paul puts it, 'For everything that was written in the past was written to teach us, so that through endurance and the encouragement of the Scriptures we might have hope' (Romans 15:4).

In another of his letters (known as epistles) he writes, 'These things happened to them as examples and were written down as warnings for us, on whom the fulfilment of the ages has come' (1 Corinthians 10:11).

Thus we interpret the Old Testament in the light of the coming of Jesus and as those who have been brought into a new covenant (relationship) with God. It is as if the train journey from the Old Testament has today to go through the hub that is 'Jesus Central'. You cannot expect to make sense of the Old if you don't make that journey. I have tried to demonstrate this in the comments made in the Old Testament section, and hope it will save you from misunderstanding which can come if you use a different route.

So, if you are a believer in Jesus, these are your books. This is your family tree. If you are not yet a believer in Jesus, I hope these readings will stir your heart to discover the wonder of God for yourself and an increasing hunger to know Him better.

HOW TO USE THIS BOOK

- Aim to set aside fifteen minutes a day to read the Bible passage for the day and the comments. Please read the Bible first; the comments assume that you have read the text. Some days will include a longer reading than others.

- Read the text prayerfully. The Holy Spirit delights to speak as we read the Word He inspired. You will certainly benefit from what He says, before reading the comments.

- Make notes as you go. You will benefit more if you write and/or underline as well as read. Make the book your own. If you have questions, write them down. They may be answered in later readings. If they aren't, they will give you some fun exploration at the end of the sixty days.

- Use the questions at the end of the day to prompt your thoughts and prayers. If you are reading the book with others, the questions will provide a discussion starter.

OLD TESTAMENT TIMELINE

		2000 BC		1500	
EDEN	EXIT	ELECTION	EGYPT 400 YEARS	EXODUS	ENTERING
Day01 Day02	Day03 Day04	Day05		Day06 Day07 Day08	Day09 Day10 Day11
Creation	Fall	Abraham		Law given	Canaan

NEW TESTAMENT TIMELINE

6 BC to AD 30–33	**AD 33**		**35**
EMMANUEL	EASTER	ECCLESIA	EVANGELION
Day31–39	Days40–45	Day46	Day47, Day56
Gospels describe Jesus' life	The final week Trial, Crucifixion, Resurrection 40 days of appearing Ascension	Coming of the Spirit at Pentecost	Gospel to Gentiles Paul's conversion

Approximate dates/time period for each day's reading

1000			500			400 Inter-testamental period 400 YEARS
EMPIRE	EMPIRE	EMPIRE DIVIDED	EXILE			EXPECTATION
			PRE-EXILE	EXILE	POST-EXILE	
Day12 Day13 Day14 Day15	Day16 Day17 Day18 Day19	Day20	Day21 Day22 Day23	Day24 Day25 Day26 Day27	Day28 Day29 Day30	
David	Temple	Decline	Prophets Assyrian Exile (722 BC)	Prophets Babylon (586 BC)	Prophets	

Approximate dates/time period for each day's reading

50	55	60	70	85
			ESCHATOLOGY	
Day48–50	Day51–53	Day54–55, Day57		Day58–60
Jerusalem Council	Nero's persecution of the Church	Paul imprisoned in Rome	Fall of Jerusalem Execution of Peter and Paul Gospels written?	John exiled on Patmos

Additional background material is available free online at: **www.cwr.org.uk/cover2cover**

Introduction to the Old Testament

This Testament covers vastly more time than the New. It starts at the beginning of creation – the date is not specified in the text – through to the time of Abraham, who is believed to have lived around 2000–1850 BC, and then via the Exodus (dated at 1500 or 1350 BC), through King David (1000 BC) to the Assyrian Exile (722 BC) and Babylonian Exile (586 BC). The canon of the Old Testament concludes around 400 BC, leaving a gap of some 400 years before the start of the New Testament era.

The events of the Old Testament centre on the Ancient Near East, including stories from Babylon in the east, Egypt to the west and the majority focused on the land of Canaan at the eastern edge of the Mediterranean Sea, the confluence of many of the world's major trade routes in the day.

In the selected passages we will focus upon, the unfolding story of God's purposes shows His choice to overturn the folly of Adam and Eve's rejection of Him, by a programme of restoration that will centre on His promises to one man, Abram (later Abraham). God promises that through him and his descendants all peoples on earth can know a special relationship

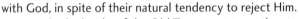

with God, in spite of their natural tendency to reject Him.

As such, the books of the Old Testament trace the stories of Abraham's descendants, who become the nation of Israel and allow us to get to know what this God is like – stories which, properly understood in the light of Jesus Christ, will give us a record of the holiness, majesty, power and kindness of the Maker of all things, and His desire to draw us close to Himself.

The Old Testament is a library of thirty-nine books. The underlying story-line can be gleaned by books regarded as 'prophetic history' by the compilers. But the Old Testament includes other kinds of literary genre that display the life and faith of the nation: law, proverbs, poetry, prophecy, songs, hymns, parables and apocalyptic writing (a highly symbolic form of writing).

The Old Testament is a terrific story of God's mighty power and dealings with His people. But it is also a very sad story, as we discover the ways in which God's intentions for His people are thwarted by their wickedness. All of this leads to the coming of God Himself in Jesus in order to do what sinful humanity cannot do on its own: shine for Him in the world.

Day[01]

READ: GENESIS 1:1–2:3

A young curate asked his vicar for some advice prior to preparing for his maiden sermon, and was told, 'Make it about God and make it about twenty minutes!'

Our opening verse reminds us that the Bible – this library of sixty-six books – is about God. He is the One who created the world and He will be the prime mover in the passages we consider over these sixty days.

This account of creation stands in stark contrast to other notions that were circulating in the Ancient Near East (an area that equates to the Middle East today). Genesis 1 is probably written to counter these myths and establish that the God of Israel created the heavens and the earth, and had a destiny and purpose for human beings within the created order.

This first chapter is written in poetic language, with the creation organised in two parallel groups of three. In the first group 'regions' are created: night and day, firmament (and atmosphere) and oceans and the land. In the second group, the corresponding inhabitants of these regions are created: astronomical bodies, birds and fish, land animals and man. So day four fills in what is formed in day one, day five fills in what is formed in day two and day six fills in what is formed in day three.

Each creature plays a part in creation, and every part is declared 'good'.

God rests on the seventh day, not because He is tired but to give a pattern of work and rest for the humans He created.

Notice that God's creative work climaxes in His creation of human beings to be like Himself (see vv.27–28). Theologian G.K. Beale suggests the Garden of Eden was like a temple of God's presence and Adam was the first priest whose job was to spread the boundaries of God's presence until the Garden filled the entire earth.* The number seven is often used in temple accounts from the ancient world, so perhaps the seven-day structure of Genesis 1 is related to the idea of temple building and inauguration ceremonies.

So, it was God's intention that Adam and Eve's children would also live under His rule, and so effectively extend the boundaries of Eden (ie His rule) through their devotion to Him. 'Subduing the earth' implies the need to rule over the created world. The more people there are in right relationship with God, the greater the impact of their leadership. The process would (in an ideal world) continue until the entire earth was covered with the glorious rule of God.

Christians have puzzled over what is meant by the words 'image of God' (v.27). Some believe that our essential characteristics as humans are derived from what He is like. We think, we feel, we choose, we relate, we have a spiritual nature, just like God. Whether we acknowledge God or not, the Genesis account states that everyone we ever meet, whatever they have done, is made in God's image. As the Bible drama unfolds we find many similarities between God and ourselves, helping us to understand what this resemblance really means.

It is clear from our reflections that the debate over what Genesis 1 tells us about how God created the world and how old the earth is misses the point. It was never the intention of the author to present a detailed scientific account. Instead we rejoice in what it reveals of the heart of our God – that He is a loving Creator who has placed us in a primary role within His creation to work with Him, even today.

QUESTIONS TO PONDER

Do you see yourself as someone made in God's image? What does this mean for you today?

*G.K. Beale, *The Temple and the Church's Mission: A Biblical Theology of the Dwelling Place of God* (Nottingham: IVP/Apollos, 2004) pp.66–80.

Day02

READ: GENESIS 2:4–25

In Genesis 1 we have an overview of the six days of the creation process. Chapter 2 is a close-up of the sixth day when Adam and Eve were created, showing us that these are the creatures who are of most importance to God as His image bearers.

Adam is told to take care of the garden and name the animals. God gives Adam jobs to do, showing His intention to partner with us in His work in the world. Whether you are a fan of gardening or not, it's clear that 'work' is given for our good before Adam and Eve sinned. Work generally has a bad press today. Some overwork or make their work too important. Some are in what they regard as 'dead end' jobs. God's intention is that we each work in ways that interact with the rest of the created world for the good of society. For many, this will take the form of paid employment (and not all jobs are, of course, directly connected to creation); others will engage in unpaid work such as bringing up a family, volunteering or making the most of retirement.

This chapter also expands on how man and woman were created, how they are distinct from each other and how they are to relate to one another.

God created Adam first and then became aware that he was lonely and needed a 'helper' (v.18), yet none of the animals was suitable. So Eve was created from Adam's rib, indicating the intimate connection between the two. Eve's role as helper to Adam does not imply subordination. Theologian Andrew Perriman has pointed out that the word for 'helper' in Hebrew is typically used in the Old Testament to refer to God, who is Israel's 'helper' in times of trouble.* The word describes a person who runs to the aid of another in difficulties. The helper must be a 'counterpart' or an 'opposite' to the man. The animals, which like Adam are made from the ground, do not meet this requirement, and it looks as if the phrase 'helper suitable' points forward to the marriage relationship, where the woman is a proper 'counterpart' to the man because the woman is 'bone of my bones and flesh of my flesh' (v.23). Words typically quoted at wedding ceremonies are found here: '... a man will leave his father and mother and be united to his wife, and they will become one flesh' (v.24).

The institution of marriage has taken a battering in recent years. This passage highlights God's intention that man and woman unite, with Him at the heart. This is not the pathway for all – notably Jesus, the most complete human who ever lived, never married – but it is the pathway for many. Marriage is also a metaphor used to communicate to the people of God in both Testaments the love that God has for them.

QUESTIONS TO PONDER

What work is there for you at present? Do you see it as something that is 'good' and from God?

*Perriman discusses this on his site: www.postost.net/2012/01/helper-fit-him

Day 03

READ: GENESIS 3:1–24

God as Creator decided what humankind would be like and also set the boundaries within which they were to operate. Within the wonderful Garden of Eden in which Adam and Eve lived, they were not to eat from the tree of the knowledge of good and evil, which was in the middle of the garden. They were told that if they ate from it they would die. It seems that God didn't want 'robots', forced to be His regardless. He wanted people who chose to follow His ways. By submitting to God, Adam and Eve would learn the joy of living as trustful and dependent creatures. This is still God's pattern for wise living today.

But this chapter starts with what seems an unusual twist – a talking snake who challenged God's prohibition, claiming that God's intentions were not good and that He was preventing Adam and Eve from fulfilling their potential.

The conversation's significance cannot be overplayed. The serpent sowed the seed of doubt about the goodness of God, a lie which we have all fallen for from time to time, and which had grave ramifications for Adam and Eve and all born into the world. This sin of not trusting God causes an immediate spiritual death in the close relationship that Adam and Eve enjoyed with God, to be followed many years later by physical death.

Most theologians see the serpent as Satan, a significant figure who appears occasionally within the biblical drama. Satan is a fallen angel who was thrown out of heaven when he sought to become an equal with God (see Revelation 12:3–9 and Isaiah 14:12–17). The irony in the drama is that Adam and Eve were made in God's image with significant prospects, but fall for the lie from one who sought greater position. Satan's opposition to God and His purposes is an underlying current that stretches throughout the Bible, even if his work is not always explicitly described. His actions come to more prominence in the New Testament, where he is variously described as 'the tempter', 'the father of lies', 'the adversary' and 'the accuser'. When Jesus died and rose again, He was victorious over him, and gave notice that Satan will one day face final judgment (cf. Revelation 20:7–10 describes his eternal separation from God's restored creation).

When Adam and Eve believe the lie of the enemy, they empower him and forfeit their relationship with God. Their single task of representing God and governing God's garden was radically distorted. As a result, God banished them from Eden.

When we believe the lies of Satan we effectively empower him and move away from God's good intentions for us.

We will discover as we move through the Bible narrative that God chooses to restore His creation once again, not by directly intervening and wiping out Satan, but by working through a community of His worshippers who will discover that God's reign is mightier than anything Satan might attempt. Many see a hint of what God will do in verse 15, when part of the curse of the serpent includes the words, 'And I will put enmity between you and the woman, and between your offspring and hers; he will crush your head, and you will strike his heel.' The 'serpent crusher' is Jesus, who would in His life, death and resurrection become the head of a new humanity, modelled after Him and not Adam.

The Bible affirms time and time again that God is good and has our best interests at heart. We will not fully understand all the nuances of His programme of restoration, especially His timing, but we can today know that the loving Creator of all is not about to forget us.

QUESTION TO PONDER

Do you believe that God has your best interests at heart?

Day04

READ: GENESIS 7:1–24 & 9:1–17

With Adam and Eve banished from the garden, sin continues to work like a virus in their lives, and in the lives of their offspring. The first murder comes when Cain murders Abel after Abel's sacrifice to God is accepted. As time passes God regrets ever making human beings and intends to wipe out the human race, together with the animals and birds, by causing a worldwide flood. We don't know the timeframe, only that God had been very patient. Some see a clue in the death of Methuselah. He was the oldest man in the Bible at 969, and his name means 'When he dies, judgment'. It was not long after Methuselah died that God sent the Flood, suggesting that God waited maybe 1,000 years before acting.

There was, however, one man, Noah, who found favour in the eyes of the Lord, so he was to be rescued together with his family. He was to build an enormous ark to contain not just the family but livestock too. Noah is obedient to God's instructions, and these chapters record the Flood and God's covenant with Noah and all humankind.

The stark description of judgment tells us how much God is grieved by sin. The God of the Bible is not an impassive being, but is described as having emotions just like us. The Flood is a permanent reminder that judgment is God's prerogative – and can be seen issued to both individuals and nations. At the final judgment all peoples will stand before Him. But, as theologians say, God's wrath is His 'strange' work. We relate to God as One who is holy and just and who must punish sin, but who in grace makes a way for us to relate to Him. Christians can know relationship with Him in Christ through the indwelling Spirit.

Chapter 9 speaks too of the preciousness of human life. Despite God's verdict on humanity, they are still 'image bearers' (v.6). God's mandate for humans to 'fill the earth and subdue it', which was given in chapter 1, is repeated in 9, verse 1 – though now roast dinner can be on the menu as the task is carried out.

But alongside judgment comes hope. God chooses to preserve the world because He intends to restore it, and makes an 'everlasting covenant' with Noah and his descendants. Noah stands as a figure who receives God's grace. He and his family are preserved for blessing. In the next part of Genesis we will see God's plans for restoration. 'New creation' will be a key motif within the narrative of the Bible, culminating in the coming of Christ and the sending of the Spirit in the New Testament.

So, although in some ways gloomy, these chapters ultimately speak of hope. In spite of God's sadness that He had made mankind, He continues with His plans to restore all things, and so offers hope to those who chose relationship with Him. God makes a covenant with Noah that He will never flood the earth again. The rainbow is the symbol to remind Him (interestingly, not us) that this agreement is lasting. His plans remain right on track.

QUESTION TO PONDER

What is the first word that comes into your mind when you think about God – angry, just, loving or something else?

Day05

READ: GENESIS 12:1-9 & 15:1-21

Chapters 9 to 11 show that far from Noah being the start of a new humanity, his descendants are really no better than those who perished in the Flood. This culminates in chapter 11, where we read of their attempt to build a tower up to God – a graphic symbol of the desire to 'be like God', which was at the root of the sins of Adam and Eve, and is still within the human heart. God reacts in judgment, forcing the peoples to speak a number of different languages, so that collusion would be impossible thereafter.

Chapter 12 represents a major turning point in the biblical story. Following the disastrous episode of the Tower of Babel, Abram is called by God to be the lead player in the next part of God's plan that will eventually lead to the coming of Jesus and our own salvation, if we want to be counted in.

This promised plan has two parts: out of all peoples God chooses this one man, Abram, who would become Abraham (see Joshua 24:3). God would make this man into a great nation and give that nation a land and bless the people. Then, God would extend that blessing to all nations (see Genesis 12:1–3; 18:18). The word 'bless' refers to life enjoyed in a relationship with God. At this stage God works with Abram and his descendants, who would become the nation of Israel. But one day, a descendant of Abram, Jesus Christ, would enable all nations in the world to know such a relationship.

We know how things turned out, but Abram is faced with a stark choice regarding whether he believes the promise of God, or not. He is in Ur (modern-day Iraq), hundreds of miles from God's intended destination in Canaan. He is old (seventy-five) and his wife is barren, so the thought of any descendants seems impossible.

As if to confirm His promise symbolically, chapter 15 describes how God commits Himself to Abram in a special covenant, or treaty. Just as surrounding nations made treaties with each other, so God makes one with Abram, while he is asleep! Then God repeats His promise that the land will one day belong to his descendants.

When the early Christians were trying to figure out what it meant to be a follower of Jesus, one of the Early Church leaders, Paul, looked back to the example of Abraham (as he became known). He reminds his readers and listeners that God accepted Abraham on the basis of his willingness to believe what God said, and that He accepted them in the same way. For us today, faith comes as we read, accept and act upon God's Word. As we put our confidence in Christ's life, death and resurrection, we are included in the blessing that was promised to Abraham. So when God was addressing Abraham, he had you and me in mind. Wow.

QUESTIONS TO PONDER

Have you ever had a moment when you believed God was asking you to do something that seemed strange? How did you respond?

Day06

READ: EXODUS 11:1–9 & 12:1–50

It's time for some 'back story' before we focus on today's passage. By the start of the book of Exodus, God's promise that Abraham's descendants would have their own land seemed to be in danger of never being fulfilled. The people were marooned in Egypt, hundreds of miles from Canaan.

Jacob (Abraham's grandson), renamed 'Israel', is the heir to the promise of God, but he has to travel to Egypt with his twelve sons when famine in Canaan puts the family's life in jeopardy. They remain in Egypt for some 400 years, and things become very difficult when the Egyptian leader (the Pharaoh) fears that the Israelites (as they were known), who now number two million, might rise up against Egypt. So he enslaves the Israelites and kills off all male babies at birth. But the people have a memory of the promise of God. They will not accept that slavery is their destiny and cry out to God. He hears their cry and raises up a Hebrew boy, Moses, who will eventually lead them out of slavery.

Moses should have lost his life at birth following the Pharaoh's edict. God's hand is seen in the way Pharaoh's daughter notices the baby Moses floating in a basket on the Nile and opts to raise him in her court. Moses would be educated as an Egyptian and would learn to write, and thus be able to record the stories of Israel later on.

But Moses had fled Egypt after he killed an Egyptian slave master. In the lead-up to our passage Moses had spent the last forty years as a shepherd. God encounters Moses by speaking from a burning bush and reveals His name – YHWH (we typically add vowels to make 'Yahweh'). The name probably means 'the ever present one'. Crucially, He is revealed as the God of Abraham, Isaac and Jacob – ie the God of the promise.

Moses, with his brother Aaron, is sent to confront Pharaoh, the leader of the superpower, telling him that God demands that he let His people go, that they might worship Him. Pharaoh refuses, and so a series of plagues is visited on the Egyptian people.

Many believe the plagues were to counter the various gods of the Egyptians. At the end of each plague, Pharaoh relents, but then changes his mind. The text tells us that Pharaoh hardens his heart (Exodus 7:13,22; 8:15,32; 9:7) and then God hardened his heart (Exodus 10:20).

In Exodus 11, God promises an intervention that will lead Pharaoh to allow the people to leave. The angel of death will take the firstborn of every household, but the Israelite firstborn are preserved, providing they follow God's instructions to slaughter a lamb and sprinkle the blood on the doorframes of their houses.

This exodus from Egypt would be a defining moment in the history of Israel – like the D-Day landings in British history. In the future, God would be referred to as 'the God who rescued you from slavery'. The Israelites would keep a feast, the Passover, each year to celebrate their liberation – a feast which Jesus would use as symbolic of the rescue He would provide through His death and resurrection, remembered by Christians today in eating bread and drinking wine at Holy Communion.

The imagery for us today is quite clear. You and I can live in the knowledge that we are freed from the power and penalty of sin that holds us in bondage. It need not have any hold over us, however powerful it may seem. We are people of freedom.

QUESTIONS TO PONDER

Have you ever wondered how God's promises to you would be fulfilled?

How do you live in the light of knowing you are free in Christ?

Day 07

READ: EXODUS 19:1–25 & 20:21

The journey from Egypt to Canaan (the land God promised to Abraham) is not without its challenges. Pharaoh changes his mind about letting the people go, and chases them. God leads the Israelites to cross the Red Sea, which miraculously parts to allow them safe passage, and then swamps and drowns the Egyptian army when they try to follow.

The people gather at Mount Sinai in the desert southwest of Canaan, and discover the awesome God who has rescued them. He asks them whether, as rescued people, they are up for the task He has assigned them – to be a kingdom of priests who serve God. This nation is to be built up in order that it will be a model community which trusts God and lives in His ways before the nations around, which were at that time enslaved by their following of other gods. Some speculate that the Israelites' time in Egypt enabled them to grow strong numerically for the task ahead of them.

The people choose to commit themselves to living as God's faithful people.

The order of events in Israel's recent history is important. Here is a people rescued from slavery who respond to God's offer of relationship. God gives them the Ten Commandments to explain how to live. It's a 'charter for freedom'. Many would argue that they encapsulate the kind of society most sensibly minded people would want to enjoy today.

Divorced from their context, keeping the laws can be mistaken as a way to get into God's good books. But the people to whom these laws are given are a rescued people – they are already in 'the book' (see Revelation 21:27)! Today we continue to value the Commandments, but can do so knowing that Jesus has kept them fully on our behalf and empowers us to become the kind of people who naturally do what the Law requires.

Whatever happens within Israel's history later, this passage explains her intended identity: as a light to the nations. God's blessing is given that we might channel it to others.

Adam was to be an image bearer who would spread God's rule; Abraham is told that he would bless all nations one day. The Church today exists that the light received through Jesus might shine into the darkest places in society. God chose to work in and through a community that would know His holiness, depicted in the fireworks and power surrounding the mountain. Later God would lead them to build a tabernacle, a portable sanctuary that would symbolise God's holiness amongst them, and in which sacrifices would be made to cover their sin. This image would be given fresh life when Jesus came and 'tabernacled with us'. God asks us the same questions He asked Israel. 'Will you be my representatives in the world? Will you obey what I say?' Our destiny, as that of Israel, is tied up in our answer.

QUESTION TO PONDER

How would you answer God's questions towards the end of the comment above?

Day 08

READ: NUMBERS 13:1–33 & 14:1–45

The march into Canaan stalls. God has miraculously rescued the people from the hands of the superpower, Egypt. His promises are on track, but as they get to the edge of the land they are to inhabit (which was about the size of Wales), the spies come back with mixed reports about their ability to take the land. Ten spies return fearful about the quality of the armies they would face and, it would seem, exaggerate their threat so that the people of God become convinced that they are going to die. Somehow a return to slavery in Egypt seems attractive. It is only Joshua and Caleb, the remaining two spies, who are convinced that God has promised them the land, and therefore they should advance. All the spies saw the same enemy and terrain, and yet it was only Joshua and Caleb whose reaction depended on what God's Word said. Is God good and faithful to His promises? If His Word shapes our life then we are better able to face the apparently insurmountable challenges.

So powerful is the word of the ten spies, they even speak of stoning Joshua and Caleb for believing God's Word. God comes to Moses and tells him that maybe it would be better if His people were wiped out and they start again, this time with Moses as the patriarch. It is an extraordinary episode.

Moses intercedes on the people's behalf reminding God that if He did that, it would undo all the good of the rescue from Egypt and would therefore reflect badly on Him. Moses asks God to forgive the people's doubts and so God relents. However He does stipulate that none of the current generation will ever enter the inheritance of the land, apart from Joshua and Caleb, who had believed Him. The faithless would wander in the desert for forty years.

The story is a very poignant and graphic picture of what happens when we ignore God's Word and direction for our lives. Thankfully, God gives us many chances, but there comes a time when ignoring a clear direction will mean that we as individuals, and indeed as churches, can effectively wander around in circles.

The picture of God in this episode may seem a surprising one to some. Did not God have a clear destiny in mind for His people? If so, why would He say that He would wipe them out and start again? As we read the narrative of the Bible we find a God who responds to His people. He is so powerful that wiping out the Egyptians, or sending a plague to wipe out His own people, is easy work. But He is also one who listens to Moses, relents and goes with a different plan. You could say that God intended to do this all along and knew what Moses would say before he said it. Maybe. But I suspect we are better to go with the text and remember that, small as we are, and as apparently insignificant as we are, God is still keen on working *with us* to further His purposes. At times that even means listening to us and changing His plans.

QUESTION TO PONDER

What parts of God's Word are you finding it hard to believe today?

Day09

READ: JOSHUA 1:1–18

Moses dies and hands on the leadership of the people of Israel to Joshua. He is now the one to lead the people into the land of Canaan – the land promised to Abraham. The promise of the land is mentioned some fifty times in the book of Joshua. Joshua is told not to be afraid and to keep the Law of God. Surprising words maybe, as he is a fighting man, but the advice does not concern clever swordsmanship or tactical acumen. Instead he is to keep his heart close to God by obeying what God had told the people.

Anyone keeping a note of where God's people have been led to up until this point might be surprised. God leads Abraham to Canaan, but, by the time of his grandson, Jacob, they end up in Egypt for 400 years, only to have to return to the land of Canaan, which is now inhabited by various peoples who will not give up the land without a fight. Joshua is promised that wherever he puts his foot, God will give the Israelites the land. This does require men that are ready for battle (v.15).

Why didn't God lead His people to another, less inhabited, part of the world where occupation would be easier?

In Genesis God actually told Abraham that his descendants would end up as slaves, to return to the land after four generations, 'for the sin of the Amorites [Canaanites] has not yet reached its full measure' (Genesis 15:16). God sees Joshua, successor to Moses, as the man to lead Israel into battle to displace the nations. Many are uncomfortable when reading this; after all, God is preparing His people to wipe out whole nations/people groups.

A little background at this point may help. The level of wickedness predicted in Genesis 15 included human sacrifice and rampant sexual practice that led to a high level of sexual disease. The people involved had to be wiped out because of likely effects upon the people of Israel. God needed to preserve His people. Throughout the Old Testament Satan used various ploys to attempt to overthrow God's people so that the line through which Jesus would come would be ended.

This was the raw struggle of a primitive people and it would seem that God communicated to them in ways they could accept. In that day, if you were victorious over your enemy, it was seen as a victory for your god. Israel understood the might of their God in His help in winning battles – with, at times, miraculous intervention.

The rest of the Old Testament would see the fortunes of God's people played out in the raw and violent times of those days (and as we look at some of the atrocities worldwide, are we any different today?).

We see in the Old Testament what is called 'progressive revelation' – God reveals Himself gradually and prepares His people for that final revelation in Jesus (Hebrews 1:1–2). These thoughts may not answer every question we have about 'horrible biblical histories', but remember that Jesus read and accepted the whole of the Old Testament. He was prepared to say that in and through His life His people today can live lives of tolerance, grace, forgiveness and peace towards all who come against them.

Just as Joshua is given the land he sets foot on, we too are called within God's kingdom to pray that everywhere we walk might have the atmosphere of God. Through prayer and spoken word, we get to be an influence for good wherever we are placed and wherever we go.

QUESTION TO PONDER

Where are you wanting to see God's rule and reign known?

Day 10

READ: JUDGES 2:1–23

The book of Judges tells the history of Israel from the death of Joshua to the rise of Samuel as the prophet of the Lord, a period of around 350 years (see 11:26; 1 Kings 6:1). In the book of Joshua are accounts of Israel's victorious conquests, including the famous fall of the walls of Jericho. But in Judges we see that for all the victories, the people of Israel are inhabiting the land of Canaan alongside the people they should have driven out: the Canaanites, Midianites, Ammonites and Philistines. It seems that a new generation had forgotten all that God had done to give them the land and were lax in their worship of Him, making covenants with other nations (1:27–36). They even joined in worship of the local people's gods, including Baal and Asherah. Under the local belief system, engaging in cult prostitution would help ensure a good season of crops.

God responded by saying that He would leave these other peoples to be 'thorns' in the side of Israel (2:1–5). This would test whether Israel would remain faithful to God or not (2:20–3:4). God remained committed to developing a model worshipping community throughout the Old Testament. He longed for His people to demonstrate His love, grace and mercy to the nations around.

The first part of Judges describes a series of repeated cycles: the people sin against God; God allows their oppressors to win; the people repent and cry out to God; God graciously sends a deliverer (a judge) who defeats the opposition and removes the altars so they know a period of peace – until they sin again.

The judges were leaders within Israel – often overseeing a more localised area – so although thirteen are listed in this book some of their reigns overlapped. The word 'judge' literally means 'establisher of justice'. Their job was to help return Israel to the ways of peace – abandoning idolatry and worshipping God alone.

The stories of the judges include some of the most rich and fascinating stories in the Bible: Gideon and 300 men against the massive Midianite army; Deborah, the only woman judge, who successfully led the Israelites against the Canaanites; and who can forget impetuous Samson, marrying the wrong woman, disobeying God yet, at the end, slaughtering thousands in a suicide mission?

As the book of Judges continues beyond Gideon, the people no longer cry out to God and things deteriorate with a bloody civil war in which the tribe of Benjamin is nearly wiped out. The overall message is clear enough – stay true to God and He will come through time and time again. Give sin a foothold and it will lead to pain and suffering.

Followers of Jesus don't typically engage in physical conflict, of course, but do face ongoing battles as they aim to live lives worthy of their King. The opposition comes from the world – typically hostile to God's ways; the flesh – our sinful nature opposes our best intentions; and the devil, who can subtly influence our thinking. We may believe that we can live with compromise, but the reality is that any harboured sin will be a 'thorn' in our side too.

We can be like the Israelites in the time of the judges, grieving and quenching the Spirit, or in Christ we can know increasing victory. Bit of a no-brainer isn't it?

QUESTION TO PONDER

What would you like God to help you overcome today?

Day 11

READ: 1 SAMUEL 8:1-21

Samuel was the last judge of Israel and became the transition figure between two periods of leadership within Israel – a tribal federation and a king who rules the whole nation. Born to Hannah, who had been barren for many years, Samuel was sent to serve the priest, Eli, and was given the ability to hear from God. He developed a reputation as a godly man and his wise counsel consistently steered Israel into God's ways.

In today's passage, the request to have a king like other nations is an outrageous snub to the God who had called them and led them as a nation. How had this small nation suffered from not having a 'king'? God was their king.

Samuel speaks to God about the request, and God passes on His answer. He points out the drawbacks of having a king. A later king, Solomon, would conscript forced labour: he used 70,000 labourers and 80,000 stone cutters to build the Temple and a royal palace for himself. The oppressed (in Egypt) became the oppressors of the people. Solomon acts just like Pharaoh did.

In 1 Samuel 9 we read how Samuel anoints Saul to be the first king of Israel. (God had pointed out the drawbacks, but does give Israel what she wants.) Anointing was both a formal act (oil was poured on Saul's head) but also a sign that God's Spirit was upon him. In the Old Testament the Spirit of God comes upon particular people for particular tasks. In the New Testament all who come to faith in Christ are given the Spirit. In Saul's case early victories are followed by disobedience. He offers sacrifice without the designated priest, Samuel, and this so displeases God that he loses the anointing. Samuel is then sent to David, a shepherd boy with no apparent credentials. For many later chapters David the anointed is on the run from Saul the king, until he is finally crowned and takes Saul's place.

In those days kings would be known as the 'son' of the deity they worshipped, and the kings in the Bible were known as 'sons of God'. Prophets would later speak of Israel as 'God's son'.

They would promise a special 'King' who would be called 'Messiah', who would be just the king that Israel always dreamed of. The messiah language was used of Jesus, though his rulership was not what they were expecting.

This switch to a monarchy would last around 500 years. With some glorious exceptions, most of the kings failed in their task of leading the people in the ways of God. But, throughout history, God remains determined to prove His faithfulness to His covenant, even when the people ignore it. He uses the concept of king-ship to demonstrate His commitment to 'kingdom'. He remains committed to having a people who enjoy His loving rule over them.

Christians today are to respect and value their leaders. But Christians will pay a price if that trust is misused. Christian leaders are followers first and will lead only as well as they stay humbly committed to God and His purposes. Jesus is potentially the leader of every church – but is He always allowed to be?

QUESTION TO PONDER

Do you pray for those who lead you?

Day 12

READ: 1 SAMUEL 17:1–58

David versus Goliath is one of the best-known stories in the Bible, used commonly today in all walks of life to describe the 'little man' overcoming the larger adversary. It's a great story that has a touch of the comic: first the young David waddling around in Saul's armour, then Goliath the giant being killed with a sling shot and his own sword. Plenty have used this narrative as a moral tale of the need to trust God when adversaries seem large. But the story in the context of 1 Samuel and the unfolding narrative gives a more powerful meaning.

At this stage in the drama, the Philistines had the upper hand in their relations with Israel, with a monopoly on weapon and machinery sharpening. We have noted already that Israel triumphs when she trusts God, and that a failure for the nation reflects badly on God. The Philistine gods were regarded as being 'stronger' on the plains, and this scene takes place in the valley of Elah. The God of Israel was deemed a hill loving deity. But this isn't just about who is best on which terrain. As David makes clear, this is about a way of living – the God you worship has moral and social connotations. We use the word 'Philistine' to describe those who do not 'appreciate certain types of art', but in those days Philistines were more profane: their worship involved sacred prostitution and possibly even child sacrifice. The people of Israel were to live God's way as a model community. Their opposition to the Philistines was an opposition to a godless way of life.

The one who would lead them in this battle and go on to become the great King David had special power – together with his skill with a sling shot. David knew his biblical history so thought: if God can overcome the Egyptian superpower then why should we fear the Philistines? At one level this is a triumph of the underdog, but it is also a triumph of the Lord's anointed – an advance of His kingdom against all the odds.

David would go on to become the most famous and valued of all Israel's kings. Under his rule, Israel would defeat the surrounding nations and extend its own borders. When Israel went into exile around 500 years later, the prophets would reassure people that God had not forgotten His promise to David that he would have a descendant on the throne. There continued to be an expectation of an 'anointed one' (Messiah) who would come. Hence the followers of Jesus were keen to emphasise His credentials as the One who as 'son of David' fulfilled and extended this provision. Matthew in particular makes this a key message in his Gospel. In the Gospels Jesus teaches that Israel had largely failed her task, but indicated He would do what she could not do and make the relationship between the Jews and their God intact once again if they would follow in His way. And He extends the same promise to you.

QUESTION TO PONDER

How would knowing that Jesus has won the victory help you right now?

Day 13

READ: 2 SAMUEL 7:1–29

Things have been going well for David and Israel. They have won important victories over Israel's enemies and the borders of the land are as great as at any point in their history. At this time, there is no temple. God's presence among the people is still symbolised in the ark of the covenant, which is housed in a tent. This seems incongruous to David, and so he shares his plans with Nathan the prophet – a respected man who has the special role of hearing from God and speaking His Word. Nathan agrees that it's a great idea and gives the green light, but he says this without asking God first and so has to return to David. The bad news is that God does not want David to build a house for Him. (He never requested this.) The good news is, in the words of Walter Brueggemann, 'one of the most crucial texts in the Old Testament for evangelical faith'*: God is going to establish a dynasty based on David's descendants. David wants to build God a house, but God will build *him* a 'house'/dynasty!

Theologians have come to call this the Davidic covenant. We have noted the Noahic, Abrahamic and Mosaic covenants, but this is the last one in the Old Testament before Jeremiah predicts the new covenant in Jeremiah 31.

Each of these covenants represents God's commitment to His people. In Noah we have a promise to Noah's descendants that He will never flood the earth again. In Abraham we have the promise of descendants, land and blessing, in order that all the nations of the world will be blessed. In the Mosaic covenant God promises that out of all the nations they will be his treasured possession – a kingdom of priests and a holy nation. This Davidic covenant extends that promise – the blessing will come to the world through the godly governance of the 'house of David'. There will always be a descendant of David on the throne and that throne will be everlasting.

At the same time God makes it very clear to David that He doesn't really need a house: the Temple is symbolic of His presence. It would become a key idea for the way the people of God would understand their role as a 'light to the nations'.

During the Babylonian Exile (586 BC) the Davidic dynasty comes to an end. The true fulfilment of the promise comes when Jesus, who was born into the line of David, is given rule over a kingdom that embraces all who truly trust Him, including Jew and Gentile (see Acts 15:16). God's intention is for all nations to be blessed through the 'son of David' – Jesus, to whom all authority is given. His kingdom is everlasting.

Today's passage shows that not every good idea is a 'God idea' – David and Nathan were incorrect in assuming that God would bless their plans. But, at the same time, God's goodness towards His people is much greater and bigger than we might imagine. His commitment to David is sheer grace, and continues despite David's infidelity, deceit and murder. Such grace is greater than your worst moments; you just need to make sure you are in a position to receive it!

QUESTION TO PONDER

Can you recall times when God has given you more blessing than you expected?

*Walter Brueggemann, *First and Second Samuel*, Interpretation: A Bible Commentary for Preaching and Teaching, ed. Patrick D. Miller, Jr. (Louisville: John Knox Press, 1990) p.253.

Day 14

READ: PSALM 23:1–6

Arranged in five books, the Psalms are Israel's hymn books, and were mostly written around the time of David, indeed many were *by* David. The songs of praise are likely to find their way into most church's Sunday worship, but in fact there are more songs of lament than praise. The Psalms reflect the breadth of life of a believer, beautifully summarised in Psalm 23, which is one of the best known and loved of all.

Although this passage does not add to the overall narrative of the Bible story, it does remind us that King David had a very personal relationship with God that he was prepared to express publicly. The king was expected to know and uphold the Law of God, even copying out the Law with his own hand (Deuteronomy 17:18). But David not only upholds the Law of God, he is also happy to lead the worship of God.

The shepherd metaphor focuses of course upon David's own livelihood prior to becoming king. This is a psalm that grows in its intimate expression – God is at first the Shepherd, spoken of in the third person: 'he makes me lie', 'leads me', 'refreshes me', 'guides me'. But, from verse 4, David refers to God as 'you', continuing the psalm addressing his words directly to God, almost like a reflective prayer of gratitude.

These are words from someone who has found God to be totally satisfying, providing at every step of the journey, including times when facing opposition (v.5), and who is confident of His provision even when death itself comes close (v.4). He proves God's faithfulness in the wilderness as a shepherd, as a young warrior against Goliath, on the run from Saul and now as the leader of Israel.

Not everyone in Israel would have had David's personal faith, but the psalm does remind us of the kind of relationship that can be expected by believers in God. The Psalms have been so valued by the Church because they express the varied emotions in life: the pain of those who feel God is nowhere, the anger of those who feel God has let them down and the joy of those who discover that nothing compares with the close relationship that they can enjoy. Those singing the psalter are thus drawn to express words about a closeness to God that they might not necessarily feel now, but aspire to, pleased that, whatever the quality of their walk, there is more to know and enjoy.

Jesus would go on to remind us in John 4:24 that the Father seeks worshippers, and that those who worship Him must worship Him 'in spirit and in truth'. The passion expressed in the Psalms reminds us we are not to be rule-keeping robots, doing our duty day after day, but people who genuinely 'love' the Lord our God with all our hearts, souls and strength (Deuteronomy 6:5).

QUESTION TO PONDER

Are you more focused on loving devotion or rule keeping?

Day 15

READ: 2 CHRONICLES 6:1–42

The books of Chronicles cover a similar period to that of 2 Samuel and 1 Kings, and this passage is almost identical to one in 1 Kings. Surely there must be some mistake! But just as we have four Gospels, each looking at Jesus from a slightly different perspective, so we have two accounts of the history of Israel, each written from a slightly different viewpoint. Scholars believe Kings and Chronicles were written after the Babylonian captivity (ie after 586 BC). In the books of Samuel and Kings the authors chart the way in which Israel declines from the high point of the reigns of David and Solomon. In Chronicles, the authors are looking to a future hope within their context so some of the more pessimistic episodes recorded in Kings are not in Chronicles.

The building and dedication of the Temple had an important symbolic significance for the people of God. It would have been one of the wonders of the world at that time and, as such, provided an important demonstration of the might and power of God, bolstering Israel's role as a light to the nations around. Scholars tell us that Israel's Temple in the Old Testament points back to the Garden of Eden in the first chapters of the biblical story (Genesis 1–2) and forward to the new creation in the last chapters (Revelation 21–22). We have seen that Eden was the unique place of God's presence, where Adam and Eve enjoyed intimate fellowship with God. Adam was also portrayed as the first priest charged to serve and guard the sanctuary of God and expand its boundaries into the regions beyond. At times Israel needed to repel the nations who would have gladly wiped them out; on other occasions it is clear that their success had an impact.

The Temple reminded the people that at the heart of the nation was the presence, power and glory of God. But the concern for 'all nations' is evident even here. In verses 32 to 33, Solomon alludes to the 'foreigners' who might approach God through the Temple: '… when they come and pray towards this temple, then hear from heaven, your dwelling-place. Do whatever the foreigner asks of you, so that all the peoples of the earth may know your name and fear you, as do your own people Israel ...'

Overall, Solomon's words seem pessimistic for a dedication ceremony, but they do anticipate the trauma that Israel would undergo in the next centuries.

Sadly, what was to be a symbol of their identity as a light to the nations became a stumbling block. Although Solomon makes it clear that the heavens cannot contain God, there would be times when Israel would live as if God was *only* in His Temple. Their attitude suggested that they believed if they sacrificed animals at the right time, He would be happy with them. Christians down through the ages have sometimes linked their place of worship too closely with God, forgetting that God is to be welcomed and acknowledged in the factory, office, home and sports field, as much as in a building with pews and stained glass windows. Look around you. You are in a place of worship right now.

QUESTION TO PONDERS

Where do you think God is, really?

Where do you feel closest to God?

Has there been a time when you were going through the motions spiritually? What brought that to an end?

Day 16

READ: PROVERBS 3:1–35

Life is lived moment by moment. You probably think very little about your life's grand narrative. Most of the time your mind will be thinking about your next project. Our necessary focus on the overall story of the Bible can blind us to the real believers who were facing daily situations and wanting to remain true to God in them. Proverbs is a collection of wise sayings that helped the people of God, and help us today, to figure out how to navigate through life's challenges. This chapter alone includes topics such as trust, giving, honesty, violence, generosity, discipline and wisdom. Proverbs are not laws, but sayings about how life generally pans out when lived a certain way. They are not unlike the sayings beloved of an older generation, offered to give skill in the handling of life to those who are still learning. Proverbs reflect a God-bathed view of the world. He is as much involved in the business life as the religious, as concerned about our reaction to one another as our reaction to what He says.

The sayings from Solomon are connected to his response to God. God asked Solomon what he wanted and Solomon asked for wisdom above riches. We read in 1 Kings 4:32 that 3,000 proverbs and over 1,000 songs are said to have come from Solomon. It is also said that people came from all over the ancient world to hear the wisdom of Solomon. Along with the books of Job, Ecclesiastes and the Song of Songs, Proverbs makes up what is known as the 'wisdom literature' in our Bible.

The summaries of wisdom in this chapter are worth noting. The well-known verses 5 to 7 allude to our inherent foolishness. We can have good ideas, and think we can figure life out, but the man and woman of God who is wise will have put their total trust in God. Indeed wisdom matters so much that it pays greater dividends than owning precious metals. Other proverbs tell us that God Himself is at the heart of wisdom, 'the fear of the LORD is the beginning of wisdom' (Proverbs 9:10). This fear is an appropriate awe-filled respect for the God of the universe, whose wise dealings in our lives are welcomed.

Even having and knowing wisdom, we still need to exercise our wills in the right direction. Solomon may be the answer to the question, 'Who is the wisest man in the Bible?', but he didn't use the wisdom he had. He had a weakness for foreign women that led him away from God, and he pursued building projects that made some of the people of God effectively slaves in their own land. Like all Old Testament heroes, Solomon is flawed. Paul reminds us in the New Testament that it is Jesus who is the power of God and the wisdom of God (1 Corinthians 1:22–24). Being filled with His Spirit, Christians can know a divine wisdom for dealing with life's issues. And this includes the many decisions you will be taking as soon as you finish this reading.

QUESTIONS TO PONDER

In what situations do you need wisdom today? How will you find it?

Day 17

READ: JOB 1:1–22 & 42:1–17

Life sometimes goes pear shaped. You have trusted God, you have followed His ways. You seem to be doing all the right things and then disaster strikes, and you feel totally lousy and are left asking God, 'Why?'

The book of Job focuses on suffering through the story of a godly man who is the subject of a wager between God and Satan. The opening chapter sets the scene for us. God meets with the angels and Satan, and Satan challenges Him to allow His servant to suffer. God allows Satan to do his worst, knowing that Job will remain true to Himself. The opening chapters outline the extent of Job's loss: family, livestock and health. The bulk of the book (chapters 3–31) is a cycle of speeches between Job and three friends, Eliphaz, Bildad and Zophar. Each friend provides 'wisdom' on why Job has been afflicted, but the bottom line is that each of them has decided that he must have sinned and therefore needs to work out what he had done wrong.

Towards the end of the book, Job finally gets to address God with his complaint face to face. So why does God allow suffering? Well, God asks Job to look at the wonder of creation. God questions Job on whether he is able to create and oversee the universe, the weather systems, the stars and the animal kingdom. Job's reply comes in chapter 42, verses 5 and 6: 'My ears had heard of you but now my eyes have seen you. Therefore I despise myself and repent in dust and ashes.'

God's answer was not what Job was looking for, but he concludes that he cannot understand God's ways, but must, as a created being himself, trust that He knows best.

Many find Job a difficult book and, indeed, there are strange elements to it. Does God really have a wager with Satan and afflict his servant, or does the text lead us to assume that this is a story about a fictional person written to teach us important lessons?

A few things seem clear. The book itself is not denying that our questions about suffering are valid. The friends of

Job explore the issues and the book is in our Bible to indicate that God is happy for us to question what is going on. It also demonstrates that things are happening in the spiritual realm that we may not be aware of in the physical.

Job is vindicated and, at the end of his life, sees 'double' the blessing that he had enjoyed before. Of course, not all who suffer apparently unjustly will have their wrongs righted in this life, but if we are suffering we can look ahead to all that God can and will one day do … if not in this life, then in the one to come.

We follow Jesus – the ultimate answer to the book of Job. He is the One who suffered on our behalf, so that by faith we might one day know the end to all pain and death. And He is the One who is, even in this world, able to transform our situation and teaches us to ask that His will be done on earth as in heaven. If you find the book of Job a tad depressing, and who wouldn't, make sure that you fix your eyes, not on Job but on the ultimate Answer.

QUESTION TO PONDER

Do you allow your circumstances to affect your view of God?

Day 18

READ: ECCLESIASTES 3:1–22

Should you believe everything you read in the Bible? On one level, of course, yes! It is the Word of God. But it should be read according to the literary genre. As my colleague at CWR, Philip Greenslade, puts it, we do not read it *literally*, but *literarily*. Some parts are clearly to be taken at face value (literally), but others, like Ecclesiastes, are written in a different style. You wouldn't interpret a shopping list the way you interpret a legal document. In the same way, you need to know what you are reading. The book of Ecclesiastes is one of the wisdom books believed to have been written by Solomon, though the author simply calls himself 'the Teacher'. Parts of this chapter might seem spot on: the first eight verses are much beloved by Bible readers, but what of verse 19? 'Man's fate is like that of the animals; the same fate awaits them both: As one dies, so dies the other. All have the same breath; man has no advantage over the animal. Everything is meaningless.'

The key to the book is the phrase used in verse 16, 'under the sun', a phrase which is used some twenty-seven times. The author is reflecting aloud on life, a bit like an ancient form of blogging or journalling. He reflects upon his own life, his successes and failures and what he has observed, and the book contains his conclusions along the way. He reflects on the futility of trusting in wisdom, riches, power and sex to bring meaning to life.

Another key to reading this book is to realise that the word 'meaningless' can be translated as 'ephemeral' or 'passing away'. The author is not saying that life doesn't matter, just that nothing is permanent.

So, as you read the wanderings of the author, allow them to stir you to reflect on life. This is not a book in which you are expected to 'believe every line', but rather to think about how you see the world.

The first eight verses of our reading suggest that certain activities are appropriate at certain times. If life was only about a certain one of these actions, it would be unhelpfully skewed; but we needn't feel any of them are wrong, done at the right time.

The book has been an enormous help to many today. Those who go on mental journeys like the author are surprised to find that their feelings are reflected in the biblical text.

Reading the text as Christians we can see that Christ is the answer to what Ecclesiastes longs for. In the end the author concludes in 12:13–14, 'Now all has been heard; here is the conclusion of the matter: Fear God and keep his commandments, for this is the whole duty of man. For God will bring every deed into judgment, including every hidden thing, whether it is good or evil.'

How grateful we can be today for the New Testament revelation that God has committed all judgment into the hands of One who is also our advocate, One who paid fully for our sin and welcomes us by faith into fellowship with Him.

QUESTIONS TO PONDER

As you reflect on the way you spend your time, is there anything you could do less of? Anything you could do more of?

Day 19

READ: 1 KINGS 11:1–40

Solomon is a mixture: he is believed to be the author of some of Proverbs, and the books of Ecclesiastes and Song of Songs, yet, despite being given wisdom by God, he is also very foolish.

In Deuteronomy God warned Israel that if it had a king he would tax the nation, build the military and make them slaves. There is evidence that Solomon did this. The people that had once been slaves are treated as slaves again under his rule.

Furthermore, Solomon's marriages to foreign women led him to worship other gods. The worship of Chemosh and Molech is described as detestable. Both required the sacrifice of humans to appease their wrath. Palestinian excavations have uncovered evidences of infant skeletons in burial places around shrines to Molech. A nation that was supposed to be a 'light to the nations' was led into practices that were totally against God.

People are God's image bearers, not commodities to be killed at the capricious whim of a pagan deity. But the builder of the Temple, the one who utters the prayer of dedication, is seduced by his wives into adding the worship of their deity to that of his own. God is not impressed, telling Solomon that because of his syncretistic practices he will split the kingdom, and that it is only the memory of David that stops Him from doing it there and then.

The reason for the split comes when Solomon's ambitious building projects earn him a reputation as an oppressor, and it is this aspect of his nature that costs the people. In the next chapter we read that when Rehoboam comes to the throne he continues the oppressive practices of his father Solomon, leading most of the tribes to rebel against his rule and elect another king. Judah and Benjamin in the south would be ruled in Jerusalem by Rehoboam, a territory known as 'Judah' and the other ten tribes in the north by Jeroboam, known as 'Israel'. The nation called by God through Moses was permanently split in two at this point.

At various parts of Scripture we see God at work in the free choices of people. So, just as in the days of the judges, God raises up opponents to show Solomon that ignoring His Law will not go unpunished.

The books of Kings now chronicle the lives of the kings of the two divided nations, Judah and Israel. There are some temporary revivals back to the ways of God, notably under kings Josiah and Hezekiah. But the general drift is towards the worship of foreign gods, which included cult prostitution. This is an unpleasant part of the narrative – not one commonly selected in children's Bibles! But this comes as a salutary reminder that temptation to follow alternative gods can still come to those who know God's Word inside out. Bible knowledge, in itself, is no guarantee that we will remain true to God. As my old pastor used to say, it's not how often we go through the Bible that counts, but whether the Bible 'goes through us'!

QUESTIONS TO PONDER

Solomon did not follow the Lord completely. Who of us can say that we truly do? But though we all err, there are times when we deliberately go against God. Are you doing so at the moment? If so, what do you think you should do about it?

Day 20

READ: 1 KINGS 18:1–46

God is not impassive when His people drift away from His ways. He sends His prophets (spokesmen), who typically remind the people of God that they have strayed from the covenant that they made with God on Mount Sinai, and urge them to repent and return to Him. The 'book prophets', as they are known, come at the end of the Old Testament (Isaiah to Malachi). These books record the prophecies and prophetic actions of many of the prophets. In today's account we read about the greatest of the non-book prophets, Elijah: a man who would be revered as one of Israel's finest.

At this time, the people of Israel are in a sorry state. Ahab marries a woman from Phoenecia, Jezebel, and worships Baal alongside her. Elijah is sent to declare to Ahab that God is withholding rain as punishment. Of course drought in that society, which lived by the productivity of the crops, would mean potential starvation for many. God promises that if Israel will return to Him He will be gracious, but warns that if the nation continues to rebel He will bring judgment and finally send them into exile. This passage comes at the end of the drought.

Elijah believed it was time to stop the people dithering between two gods, and tells Ahab to summon the people of Israel to Mount Carmel, in the north of the country, for a contest between God and Baal. Ahab has sufficient respect for Elijah to do as he asks and so the sacrifice is set up. Elijah pours water on his altar to establish that what he is doing is not a trick. The people watch and wait to see who will answer with fire.

Of course Baal has nothing to offer. It is the God of Israel who answers by fire. This is a unique and unusual event. There are many times in Israel's history where God displayed His glory, but this event had a particular drama and would be recounted as a major sign of God's concern that the people know that He is the Mighty One who wants the covenant be kept.

In the Gospels, we read of a time when Jesus Himself meets with Elijah, along with Moses, on the Mount of Transfiguration. Many believe that in this miraculous encounter Elijah represents the prophetic writings and Moses, the Law. Christians trust in a God who intervenes in power. The apparent power of other gods is no match for Him. This is an important lesson. Israel is reminded time and time again that it is possible to resist the powers of the other gods. The people's disobedience is down to them, not the apparent power of Baal and Asherah.

In the New Testament Satan is depicted as a real foe; we need to take up the armour of God to stand against him, and are exhorted to 'put to death whatever is of the earthly nature'. Like Israel of old we have choices. Today you and I can choose the God of Israel, the God and Father of our Lord Jesus Christ and, as and when we do, who knows what the day will bring?

QUESTION TO PONDER

Whom do you choose to follow today?

Day 21

READ: JONAH 1:1–17

Jonah is one of the strangest of books of the Bible, and the fact that a big fish swallows the prophet is the least of it. It is also one of the most important books for understanding God's intended purpose for Israel.

The prophet, who was supposed to hear God and then say what He says, ignores His command to speak to Nineveh and heads west, in the opposite direction to where he had been sent. He boards a ship that is caught in a storm. It is the pagan sailors who encourage him to cry out to God. It is they who exhibit an appropriate fear of God. Jonah asks the sailors to throw him overboard, believing this would save the crew, and it is still they who call out to God. Jonah sinks to the floor of the ocean and is swallowed by a big fish (not technically a whale, despite common understanding) and is inside it for three days and three nights.

When he is spewed out onto dry ground and is reassigned to his job by God, he goes to Nineveh and preaches. The people of Nineveh repent so God doesn't send the judgment that was anticipated. Most preachers would be delighted with such an outcome, but Jonah gets depressed and wants to die. Odd or what?

So what has this to do with the purpose of Israel? Jonah's task was to preach to the people living in the capital of the Assyrian Empire, which was the super power of the time. This is an example of a message given to the nations around Israel. Parts of the books of Jeremiah, Ezekiel, Amos, the whole of Nahum and Obadiah are addressed to the nations. On this occasion God tells the Assyrians that if they will repent He won't visit judgment on them. But the Assyrians are of course the people who took the northern tribes known as 'Israel' into exile in 722 BC, and were especially nasty in the way they fought and tortured their captives. So Jonah does not want to confront them because he knows that God might relent. Jonah would rather see them perish for what they have done. It would be like someone from Britain not wanting to preach to Nazi Germany before the end of the Second World War. Jonah is a perfect example of the person who knows what God should and shouldn't do and whom He should and shouldn't bless. Jonah, along with so many in Israel, had forgotten that their favoured status was not for bragging, but blessing. The pagan sailors and repenting Ninevites are far closer to being what God desires than the pouting prophet.

Some Christians have a 'deserving of judgment' list too. They would struggle to share a message of life with those on their list. But, like Jonah, the lesson for us all is that God is just as concerned with them as He is with us. Who are we to withhold His love and forgiveness from others? Thus Jonah is a book that testifies to God's mercy, grace and love to all peoples, and a rebuke to all who might want to pick and choose who and when people hear about Him. It also reminds us of God's commitment to the task of demonstrating His love and grace to the whole world.

QUESTION TO PONDER

Are there people with whom you would struggle to share the gospel, because you don't think they deserve it?

Day 22

READ: HOSEA 1:1–11 & 2:1–23

As we have seen, the prophets were some of the most significant people within Israel's history. The Bible includes seventeen books by people called prophets, and what we call 'history books' were regarded as prophetic history by the Jews who compiled the Old Testament. But few would sign up to be a prophet. In Hosea's case, it was one of the most emotionally testing roles in the biblical record.

One of the metaphors used to describe God's relationship with Israel is that of marriage: Israel is God's bride, betrothed to Him through the covenant on Mount Sinai (Exodus 19). Hosea is called to marry Gomer, a woman known to be unfaithful, so that he would embody within his marriage the kind of feelings that God has for His people who have ignored His laws and prostituted themselves with other gods. Hosea's life was thus a visible picture of the message he was to preach to Israel during his prophetic ministry, which was probably conducted between 747 and 720 BC. God had initiated His relationship with Israel because of His love for her. He is not an impassive judge but a spurned lover.

Of course Israel's behaviour is of no surprise to God, Gomer's immorality echoes that of the words of Moses in Deuteronomy 31:16: 'And the Lord said to Moses: "You are going to rest with your fathers, and these people will soon prostitute themselves to the foreign gods of the land they are entering. They will forsake me and break the covenant I made with them."'

Today's passage raises the prospect of a day to come when all will finally be well between God and Israel. We know that the northern kingdom does not, as a whole, heed the warnings of the prophets, and in 722 BC is conquered by the Assyrians, who scatter the people across their empire. Israel would never return to the land, unlike their southern cousins, Judah who would return after the Exile in Babylon.

In Romans 9:25–26, written nearly 800 years later, the apostle Paul quotes Hosea 2:23 (in v.25) and Hosea 1:10 (in v.26). Although these passages from Hosea refer to the spiritual restoration of Israel, Paul uses the theme to reflect on the fact that God is a saving, forgiving, restoring God. He delights to take those who are 'not my people' and make them 'my people'. Paul then applies this principle to Gentiles, whom God makes His people by grafting them into covenant relationship. All Gentile believers (you and me) have been grafted into 'the people of God'. The ten tribes of Israel may have ended in 722 BC, but God is committed to reaching all nations with His blessing – a programme that began with Abraham and, despite Israel's waywardness, is not about to be thrown off course.

This passage can therefore be seen as another sad indictment on Israei – who spurned the love of their most wonderful husband. Or you can see the passage as a massive encouragement that the God who invites us to walk with Him is not about to give up on us when we let Him down, as we often do.

QUESTION TO PONDER

How often are you reminded of God's gracious kindness to you? Think about it today.

Day 23

READ: 2 KINGS 24:1–20 & 25:1–30

These are bleak chapters! Just as the Exodus was to define the people of God, so the defeat of the nation of Judah would cast its shadow for many centuries. It was the practice of the Babylonians (also known as Chaldeans) to deport the people they overran and so, having conquered Jerusalem, they forced around 10,000 people to relocate to the city of Babylon, the capital of the Chaldean Empire, which was around 900 miles east of Jerusalem. It was an awful time. The king lost his sons and his sight, and the people of Judah felt as if the life of the nation had been sucked away.

After these events in 586 BC Judah itself ceased to be an independent kingdom, and the people found themselves without a homeland, without a state and without a nation. This period, which first started in 597 but is traditionally dated at 586, is called 'the Exile' in Jewish history (though there was another, Assyrian, exile in 722 BC).

The deported people would include Daniel and his friends, Shadrach, Meshach and Abednego (all mentioned in the book of Daniel), who were in their late teens, as well as the priest Ezekiel, who is called to speak God's Word in Babylon (see the book of Ezekiel). But only the most prominent citizens of Judah, professionals, priests, craftsmen and the wealthy, were taken. The people living off the land were allowed to stay. Jewish history has two parts during the Exile: the Jews in Babylon and the Jews who remain in Judah. We know almost nothing of the Jews in Judah after 586 BC. Judah seems to have been wracked by famine, according to the biblical book Lamentations, which was written in Jerusalem during the Exile.

Many of the book prophets are categorised according to the Exile of the southern kingdom to Babylon: 'pre-Exilic', 'Exilic' and 'post-Exilic'. This Exile was a time of deep soul searching and reflection, aided by the exilic prophets who emphasised God's hand in allowing it to happen.

But while the Assyrian deportation of Israelites (the name for the ten northern tribes) in 722 BC resulted in the complete disappearance of the Israelites, the deported Jews formed their own community in Babylon and retained their religion, practices and philosophies. They came to realise that they had been responsible for the disaster of the Exile. In Deuteronomy 28 God had warned that if they left Him and followed other gods, He would expel them from the land. So they looked back to their Mosaic origins in an effort to revive their original faith. It is most likely that the Torah (the first five books of the Bible) took its final shape during this period, or shortly afterward, and that it became the central text of the Jewish faith at this time as well.

Believers in Jesus will know bleak times too. God does not protect us from the unpleasantness of life and the consequences of the unwise choices we make. But He promises to be with us in the pain and to weave even our mistakes into something that will be for our good and the good of those around us. Just as this period of Exile came to an end when Cyrus the Persian conquered Mesopotamia (he allowed the Jews to return home specifically to worship God), so there will be an end to our suffering. We can know respite in this world and one day in the world to come where all sorrow, death and pain will finally be over.

QUESTION TO PONDER

As you reflect on your life, have there been times when what seemed really bad actually led to the creation of good?

Day 24

READ: JEREMIAH 31:1–40

Jeremiah is called the 'weeping prophet' because so much of his message is doom and gloom concerning the behaviour of Israel. We have already noted that the Israelites had violated the covenant agreement of Mount Sinai in Exodus 19. They had broken the Ten Commandments and followed other deities. The book of Lamentations is Jeremiah's lament for the city that now lies devastated.

But parts of his prophecy are full of hope and this chapter speaks of the joy of the return to the land and of a new work that God is going to do. The nations around will see that God has brought His people back. He is being true to His covenant promise. But, more than that, Jeremiah asserts God's resolve to renew the covenant that has been broken by ancient Israel (vv.31–34). It will be a renewed covenant, but one that stands in continuity with that of Sinai. The link between the two is that both are concerned with God's Law. But, whereas the old Israel was unable to keep the Law, this new covenant will include a work within the heart so that there will be a new inclination to keep the Law.

This is a pivotal passage for the whole Bible. It is the only explicit reference to the new covenant in the Old Testament, though many other prophecies speak of the coming of Jesus and what He will accomplish, around 500 years later. In the new covenant (which could also be known as New Agreement or New Testament) Jesus deals fully and finally with the sin that separates Israel from God, and by His Spirit enables them to be the kind of people that keep God's Law. His death is commemorated during Communion and Jeremiah 31:31–34 is quoted in the New Testament, as the writer of Hebrews in chapter 8 reflects on the wonderful new thing God has done.

Under the new covenant, non-Jews are now welcomed into the family of God. The Ten Commandments are still valid, but two things have happened. First Jesus has kept the Law fully on our behalf. His was a sinless life. Through trusting Him, we can be those who are declared 'not guilty', even though we fail to keep the Law. Secondly, God is at work so that we become the kind of people who naturally keep the Ten Commandments, because we have a new heart that chooses good over evil. Through faith in Jesus, God's Spirit lives within us. As we cooperate with Him, our inner motivations are turned towards God and away from sin.

Once again the Old Testament tells us of God's dealings with His people. It shows the seriousness of sin and the wonder of God's solution in Jesus. You can of course find reasons to be gloomy as you look at how the state of your life measures up against the Law of God, or you can marvel afresh at the new life by the Spirit open to those who follow Jesus. I think I know where I would focus ...

QUESTIONS TO PONDER

Do you live your Christian life with the law uppermost in your thinking? Or do you live as someone who knows God's grace in Christ?

Day 25

READ: EZEKIEL 37:1–28

Ezekiel was among the Jews that were exiled to Babylon by Nebuchadnezzar. He was married, lived in a house of his own along with his fellow Jews and, though confined to Babylonia, had a relatively free existence there.

He was of a priestly family and was eligible to serve as a priest. But this priest-prophet was called to minister during one of the most turbulent times in Judah's history, both before and during the Babylonian Exile. His prophecies include warnings to Jerusalem that they will be sent into exile if they don't repent, as well as assurances that God is with them in exile and has a future for them in spite of exile. Much of his preaching centres upon the glory of God present in the Temple, and pictured as leaving the Temple when it is destroyed in 586 BC. It assures the people that God is with them, even though they are separated from the Temple of the Lord with its symbolism, sacrifices, priestly ministrations and worship rituals.

Today's passage is one of the best known in the book, not least because of the well-known traditional 'spiritual' song 'Dem Bones', used to teach basic anatomy to children, which is based on it. Ezekiel is given this vision of a valley of dry bones and told to prophesy life and breath to them. He sees the bones come to life, receiving tendons, flesh and finally skin, and is told that this represents Israel returning to life, after exile. 'Then you, my people, will know that I am the LORD, when I open your graves and bring you up from them. I will put my Spirit in you and you will live, and I will settle you in your own land. Then you will know that I the LORD have spoken, and I have done it, declares the LORD' (37:13–14).

Later Ezekiel is told that the northern tribes (called Ephraim here) and Judah will be made one again back in the land. The northern ten tribes had been scattered during the former Assyrian Exile in 722 BC. But when the people of Judah return to the land the northern tribes are still lost. The fulfilment of this prophecy comes much later with the blessing of all the nations through Jesus. Jesus calls twelve apostles, in part symbolic of the new thing He is doing in the whole nation (symbolising the twelve tribes). At Pentecost Jewish people scattered among the nations hear the Word in their own tongue and embrace the message. The ultimate fulfilment comes when one day people of every tribe and people and nation gather around the throne.

Along with Jeremiah 31, Ezekiel 37 represents a significant marker for what God intends to do under His new covenant. The only solution for the problem of sin in human hearts is radical surgery performed by God Himself. Spiritual life comes only by the infusion with God's Spirit. Believers today have the joy of knowing God wherever they are. We are not tied to buildings, forms of worship or special places. As Dutch theologian Abraham Kuyper put it, 'there is not one inch of creation of which Christ doesn't say "mine"'.*

QUESTION TO PONDER

Think of the places you will be in the next seven days. Can you imagine God being there with you in each one?

*Taken from Kuyper's inaugural address at the dedication of the Free University.

Day 26

READ: ISAIAH 52:1–15 & 53:1–12

During the Exile the prophets spoke not just about God bringing the people back, but hinted at God doing something very different in His restoration of the people of God. These chapters speak of One who is the 'servant of God', whose life, death and resurrection will do for Israel what she could not do for herself.

Written 600 years before Jesus was born on earth, the prophet describes 'piercing' (53:5), describing the nails that would tear Jesus' hands and feet and the sword that would pierce His side at the crucifixion. Matthew's Gospel would speak of Jesus' healing ministry as fulfilling Isaiah's prophecy in verse 5, 'by his wounds we are healed' (Matthew 8:17). We find that His death is God's will, but God will vindicate Him and exalt Him. Here is One who would wonderfully intervene in Israel's affairs – greater than any of the leaders, kings and prophets who had come before.

But we miss much if we *just* look at the clear parallels between the 'Servant' and Jesus. The prophet has a wide panorama in view. He is concerned that the 'ends of the earth' see God redeeming His people, in returning from the Exile, but also in vindicating them through the life of Jesus.

Isaiah 52:7–12 can be seen to sum up the whole of Jesus' public ministry. Note verse 7: 'How beautiful on the mountains are the feet of those who bring good news, who proclaim peace, who bring good tidings, who proclaim salvation, who say to Zion, "Your God reigns!"'

When Jesus began His public ministry in Israel, He announced that the kingdom of God was at hand in His ministry. God's reign in and through Israel had been hampered by sin and then exile. Although there would be a physical return from the Exile by some Jews (many would choose to remain in Babylon), by the time of the Gospels there is a recognition that the people of God are still in 'spiritual exile'. The expectation of the prophets (including Isaiah) remained to be fulfilled.

All of this reminds us that when the Gospels start with 'the good news of Jesus Christ', the message is initially one to Israel. Mark takes us back to Isaiah at the start of his Gospel as he anticipates the coming of John the Baptist, the forerunner of Jesus. In Jesus we have One who will deal with Israel's sin problem once and for all. It is because Jesus is Saviour of Israel that He is also Saviour of the world! It is because He is now proclaimed Lord of all that we can by faith benefit from His rule and reign. This is not about subjective feelings, but an assured faith in the God who brings a Saviour to us. Jesus has 'beautiful feet' as the herald of this wonderful news.

QUESTIONS TO PONDER

What are your feet like?

How do you respond to the knowledge that various passages in the Old Testament, such as the one today, reveal Jesus to us?

Day 27

READ: DANIEL 6:1–28

This is one of the most popular children's stories in the entire Bible. It has all the elements of a classic story. The righteous hero is set up by his enemies, who are plotting his downfall. The tricked king is full of anguish during the overnight suspense wondering what will happen to God's man at the hands of ferocious beasts. Finally God's man is eventually delivered and the tables turned on the bad guys.

We have already seen that such stories are part of the wider narrative of God's dealings with His people. Daniel was one of a number of highly talented youths exiled to Babylon. The narrative part of this book establishes how Daniel and his friends remain true to God in the pagan land and ideals of Babylon. God is with Daniel and gives him the ability to interpret the dreams of the Babylonian rulers. The second half of Daniel includes a form of literature known as 'apocalyptic', which uses highly symbolic language to unveil what is going on both at that time and in the future. Many believe that Daniel was written to bolster the faith of people who were suffering persecution and were beginning to conclude that God had forgotten His promises to His people.

The moral of the story is certainly not, 'stay faithful to God and He will rescue you from what harms you', at least not in a specific sense. God does not always intervene in this dramatic way. But it is saying that all will ultimately be well if we commit ourselves to the One who can intervene and will further His purposes in the world through us. Those who take up their cross and follow Jesus recognise that their lives are heading nowhere without Him, and are enabled to stand wherever God has placed them. In some parts of the world this means living in a hostile environment. In others, such as the UK, the pressure may be subtler but is nevertheless still real. In Daniel the outcome is that the pagan king becomes aware of the greatness of God and tells his own people that they should give God due reverence. The people of God were intended to be a light to the nations; in this passage, one man's light shone and millions have had a glimpse of that light.

The book of Daniel tells how all the kingdoms of the world are eventually 'crushed' by God's kingdom. Daniel joins with other prophets to show that God's work is on track and His people *will* be vindicated for their faithfulness. One will come who will invite people to enter the kingdom of God and who will tell His followers that 'all authority in heaven and on earth has been given to me' (Matthew 28:18).

Kingdoms and empires will rise and fall, but there is an unseen work that continues as those who align themselves with Jesus become part of a rule and reign that one day will become apparent to everyone.

QUESTION TO PONDER

Have you ever stood firm for what you believed despite unpleasant consequences?

Day 28

READ: HAGGAI 1:1–15 & 2:1–23

The word 'priorities' has become a loaded word for many. We may remember being told to 'get your priorities straight' by a teacher or parent when we found play time more appealing than homework. In Haggai's prophecy, God is concerned about His people's priorities.

We have seen how God is relegated down the priority list many times in the Old Testament narrative. At this point in the story, many of God's people have returned from the Exile in Babylon to the land of Israel. God had been faithful to His promise that the Exile would last for seventy years. But exile was not the end of the nation or their occupation of the land. A remnant that had not been deported was already living in Israel, although we know very little about them. We know from the book of Ezra that the people of God had started to rebuild the Temple but had halted the work when scurrilous rumours reached the Emperor suggesting attempts to rebuild the Temple were because they wanted to revolt against Persia. Fearing punitive action from Persia they had stopped.

The prophet's job was to challenge the people about prioritising their own homes over God's. God had, in the past, withheld rain to alert His people to their behaviour. He was doing it again. The crops had been hit with blight, mildew and hail, but they hadn't thought to turn back to God.

Thankfully the word from God was heeded and the Temple was rebuilt. Haggai reports that three weeks after his first prophecy, the rebuilding of the Temple began on 7 September 521 BC: 'They came and began work on the house of the LORD Almighty, their God, on the twenty-fourth day of the sixth month in the second year of King Darius' (Haggai 1:14–15). The Book of Ezra indicates that it was finished on 25 February 516 BC (Ezra 6:15).

With prophetic encouragement from the prophet Zechariah too, there was great expectation that God's purposes for a wholesale renewal of Israel back to the heady days of King

David were to be fulfilled. But in chapter 2 Haggai tells them that this new Temple is a pale shadow compared to the splendour of Solomon's. He hints that God's glory would fill a temple one day that would be better even than the one that was destroyed in the flames. The 'desired of all nations' could be a reference to Jesus Himself, though we cannot be sure. It certainly fits with our theme that one day all the nations of the world will be blessed, and people of every tribe and people and tongue will be gathered in worship.

It is also true that everyone you meet desires Jesus, they just don't know it yet. It was an Early Church Father, Augustine, who said that there is a 'God-shaped hole' in everyone. That is even true of the people you know who have no interest in God and the gospel. Today would be a good day to pray that their hearts and minds are opened so that they know just how wonderful God's solution to their need really is.

QUESTIONS TO PONDER

Have you ever listed your true priorities in life? What place does God have within those priorities?

Are you praying for those you know who don't yet know Jesus?

Day 29

READ: NEHEMIAH 6:1–19

In Susa, the capital of the Persian Empire, in around 445 BC, Nehemiah, the cup bearer to the King of Persia, Artaxerxes I (head of the super power of the day), receives news that the walls of Jerusalem are in a dilapidated state. The Jews had been allowed to return to the land in 538 BC when Cyrus had allowed all people exiled under the Babylonians to return and many had, under the leadership of Zerubbabel. Many more had returned under Ezra, possibly in 458/457 BC. So with this number now back, Nehemiah found it unthinkable that they had not repaired the walls, which were symbolic of safety and a status within the Middle East. It was the equivalent of buying a house but leaving it with no doors and windows.

Nehemiah takes time to fast and pray and then, when an opportunity arises four months after, he asks the king for leave to return to Jerusalem to rebuild the wall. He is not only given leave, but also resources. He mobilises people in Jerusalem, sets them to work rebuilding the wall close to their own homes, and our text tells us that in just over seven weeks the walls were rebuilt. It wasn't plain sailing though. Nehemiah faced pressure from his own people, who became discouraged by threats from non-Jews in Jerusalem. In this chapter we read of the attempts of these leaders to dissuade Nehemiah from the task.

The book of Nehemiah was originally the second half of a one-volume work joined to the book of Ezra, and the rest of it charts the spiritual renewal of the people. The wall may have allowed the people to establish borders, but there was still the danger that their lives were not guarded from the unhealthy connections with other religions. In a moving prayer Nehemiah recounts the way God had led them as a people and they had rebelled. Now was the time to dedicate themselves afresh to God (Nehemiah 9:1–37).

We have seen throughout the Old Testament story that an Israel that is spiritually strong is able to shine for God.

Physical return to the land is granted by Cyrus, that they might worship their God (Ezra 1:1–4). But a people who remain focused on other gods, and have little or no recollection of the Law of God, are not in a fit state to worship at all. A spiritual renewal needed to follow on from their physical return to the land.

Nehemiah is a book that many have used to teach leadership principles, and there is certainly much to admire within it. The refrain throughout is the way God enabled the work to happen – through a benevolent pagan king and the strength and energy given to the people. As the people poured themselves into the task, Nehemiah was quick to give credit to God. If and when God gives tasks to His people, He always provides the energy for completion, and it will be clear that it was 'done with the help of our God' (Nehemiah 6:16). And the same can be true for you.

QUESTIONS TO PONDER

Is there anything that concerns you so much that it would lead you to fast? Has there ever been a time when you have known God to direct you to do something, and given you the resources and energy to do it?

Day 30

READ: MALACHI 3:1–18 & 4:1–6

The closing pages of any book are crucial to the work, especially if the story has been heading to some sort of climax. Authors that leave their readers 'hanging' need to have a very good reason. It is strange perhaps that the end of the Old Testament should finish in this way – the last word in Hebrew can be translated 'curse'! In fact, the Hebrew Bible actually finishes with Chronicles. The canon is in three sections, Torah, Prophets (the former prophets Joshua, Judges, the books of Samuel and Kings), the latter prophets (Isaiah to Malachi) and the Writings, which finish with Chronicles.

The book of Malachi itself seems to reflect conditions around the time of Ezra and Nehemiah, with some speculating that Malachi prophesied when Nehemiah was away from Jerusalem. It is structured around six disputes. Each dispute follows a consistent pattern: The issue is raised by God (eg '"I have loved you," says the LORD'). The people question God (eg 'But you say, "How have you loved us?"'). God responds by showing examples. The first three deal with Israel's second-rate sacrifices. The last three deal with Israel's doubts about God's justice.

These chapters reflect a situation that is all too common throughout the biblical story. God's people, now back in the land, have not learned their lesson from the Exile. God holds out His arms in welcome but the people remain impassive to His pleas. They appear to be puzzled that God is not blessing them (1:7; 2:14; 3:8; 3:13). They were unable to see the connection between their behaviour and God's displeasure with them (2:17).

In chapter 3 they have not fulfilled their covenantal obligation to give ten per cent of what they earned back to God. Deuteronomy 14:22–29 stated that one-tenth of all that came into their possession belonged to God. This was used for the Levites (who had no land) and the foreigners, the fatherless and the widows who had no means of income. In Deuteronomy

God promises to bless those who give back to God, and here the blessing is repeated. You cannot out-give God!

The closing chapter urges the people to return to the Law of God. The refrain 'return to God's Word' is one that has echoed down through the centuries. But there is also a hint of the future – the mention of 'Elijah' (an Old Testament prophet) returning, which the New Testament depicts as John the Baptist and 'the sun of righteousness [rising] with healing in its wings' (Malachi 4:2), a reference, many believe, to Jesus Himself.

The Old Testament closes with many prophetic words unfulfilled. The people are back in the land, but still in spiritual exile awaiting the One to whom the Old Testament points. It is perhaps a poor ending to a book, but that's because this part of the canon is but the prequel to the main attraction: Jesus Christ.

QUESTION TO PONDER

What is your response to what you have learnt from the Old Testament after these thirty days of readings?

Introduction to the New Testament

The life, death, resurrection and ascension of Jesus is central to the whole Bible and is recorded for us in four books we call Gospels (literally, 'good news') that come at the start of the New Testament. Technically they are four accounts of the one gospel of Jesus. So Matthew is known as 'The Gospel according Matthew', to emphasise that each author wrote according to their own perspective, highlighting particular elements of the Jesus story.

In all probability Mark was written first, based, according to Early Church writings, on the memories of Peter, an apostle who was especially close to Jesus. Matthew and Luke probably had the text of Mark when they wrote their Gospels, for most of Mark is in these Gospels – though each has their own material too (and some that is common to them but not in Mark). For this reason these three are known as the Synoptic Gospels. Luke's Gospel is written more as a historian might write, his Gospel being the first of a two-part work, the second being the book of the Acts of the Apostles. John was written last and in a very different style, based in part around seven 'signs' (miracles) that point to who Jesus is, and seven 'I am' sayings.

Although the Gospels are read first and cover the first three decades of the first century, they were written after most of the epistles found later in the New Testament, probably around AD 70.

This date is a pivotal one in our understanding of Early Church history. This is the date of the fall of Jerusalem and the destruction of the Temple by the Romans, an event that was predicted by Jesus and which represented God's judgment on the nation of Israel. This cataclysmic event for the Jewish people, coming forty or so years after Jesus' death, resurrection and ascension probably led to the apostles' concern that the stories of Jesus, which had been circulating orally, should be written down.

The book of Acts functions as a history book within the New Testament. It is Luke's second volume after his Gospel, written to show how the work of Jesus continues by His Spirit as thousands across the Roman world embrace the message and form communities of Christ followers.

The letters or epistles were written by the apostles (thirteen by one new apostle, Paul) to help churches and individuals grasp the implications of a faith in Christ in the light of God's dealings with His people under the old covenant – and given the challenges of the surrounding culture and philosophies that they faced. They were typically written to address particular issues that were being faced, rather than as theological treaties written in isolation. On the whole, I have selected passages from books in the same order that they appear in the Bible. Please note that the epistles are not arranged in chronological order.

The last book, Revelation, is a series of revelations given to the apostle John, who was imprisoned on the isle of Patmos at the time. These serve to strengthen the persecuted church in Asia Minor and give us a glimpse of the end of time when God completes His restoration work and brings in a new heaven and earth.

The New Testament is thus a missions-based document, pulsating with the desire of the Early Church leaders for as many as possible to learn about the coming of Christ. It is likely that all the documents were finished within the first century, possibly even the first eighty years.

Day 31

READ: JOHN 1:1–18

The New Testament begins with four complementary accounts of the life of Jesus. As we noted in the introduction to the New Testament part of the Bible, the Gospel of John was probably written last. It starts its account back at the beginning of time. 'In the beginning' before the creation of the world, 'the Word' exists. The language is reminiscent of Genesis 1:1, and this 'Word' is John's clever shorthand to help his readers appreciate that the subject of his Gospel, Jesus Christ, is no mere human, but God Himself.

God existed before the world and enjoys fellowship of love and unity within Himself. He had no need to create the world, other than a desire to glorify Himself through creating beings who would enjoy Him.

Reflection on what Scripture says about God has led theologians to state that God is One, but three distinct eternal Persons: God the Father, God the Son and God the Holy Spirit. We have seen that the Old Testament books form a narrative of God's dealings with humankind and reveal the intention of God the Son to come to earth in the womb of a woman and grow as a normal human being, while at the same time display all the wonder of God Himself. He is both fully God and fully man.

As well as positioning God the Son, Jesus, at the start of creation, this chapter also explains that Jesus is active within creation itself: 'Through him all things were made; without him nothing was made that has been made' (v.3).

Many find it helpful to think of Jesus helping execute the Father's desires with respect to creation. Scientists tell us that the diameter of the observable universe is at least ninety-three billion light years. The National Science Foundation's 'Tree of Life' project estimates that there could be anywhere from five million to a hundred million species on the planet, but science has only identified about two million. This is an immense work!

But this 'Word', Jesus, is also the One who brings human beings into connection with the Godhead. We can be 'born of God', knowing a special relationship as His children only through Jesus. John is introducing this concept to us, planning to explain more about who Jesus is in his Gospel.

The background of the language in verse 14 is that God literally pitches His tent in our neighbourhood – not to protest or be a nuisance, but display what He is like. You and I get to know what God is like through Jesus. This Gospel, indeed all the Gospels, is essential reading for anyone who wonders what God is like. What we learn of God in the Old Testament is wonderfully true, but it is in Jesus that we are left in no doubt of His character and purposes towards a lost humanity. So if you are wondering what God might be up to in a situation, ask yourself what Jesus would do? It may help.

QUESTION TO PONDER

Do you find it easy to imagine Jesus helping to create the world?

Day 32

READ: LUKE 2:1–14; MATTHEW 1:18–25 & 2:1–23

Of the four Gospels, just Luke and Matthew provide accounts of the birth of Jesus, with each focusing upon different elements. Luke explains how a Nazareth-based couple come to be in Bethlehem, in the south of Israel, for the birth of their first child and recounts the angels appearing to shepherds who visit on the night of the birth. In Matthew's Gospel, the birth narrative explores how some 'wise men' visit the child some time after the actual birth, which is consistent with Jesus' portrayal as a king within the Gospel.

We see God's activity in both accounts: in Caesar's decree that led to Joseph and Mary's journey to Bethlehem, several days' journey south of their home, thus fulfilling Micah's prophecy regarding the birthplace of Israel's special 'ruler'; in the star appearing and guiding the wise men; and, of course, supremely, in His coming to earth – the mystery of God the Son, who was pivotal in the creation of the whole universe, becoming a growing foetus in the womb of a peasant girl.

Both Luke and Matthew are concerned that we spot the way in which Christ's coming links with the story of God's people in the Old Testament. Luke records how Jesus is brought to the Temple to be circumcised (Luke 2:21) and Simeon is given insight that this One represents God's salvation – for both Gentiles and Israel (Luke 2:28–32). Anna speaks of the 'redemption of Jerusalem'. Matthew mentions that Jesus is so-named because He will 'save his people from their sins'.

Matthew contrasts 'King' Jesus, with the king of the time, Herod the Great. Herod attempts to assert his power, eventually killing all under-twos in an effort to squash what he saw as a usurper. Jesus would be a king who would give His own life to fulfil the divine purpose. The visit of the wise men, from outside Israel, signifies that all nations will eventually come to worship this One.

Matthew is keen that we link Jesus with all that God was doing in the Old Testament, referencing back nearly 200 times in his Gospel. Jesus is not arbitrarily parachuted into the world like a space man, but comes at just the right time (Galatians 4:4) to renew the people of God and enable those who would trust Him to enter their destiny as a nation to bless the world – as God had promised Abraham.

Jesus came to do what Adam and Eve failed to do – establish His rule throughout all the earth as a priest and king so that evil is overcome and the glory of God is known more and more. The rule and reign of God can be known, not in a political solution that would overthrow human oppressors, but living a new kind of life following Him.

Luke continues his account with reference to Jesus' growth as a normal human being – within a simple Nazareth home, knowing God's grace upon Him in the secret place, learning a trade from His father, until the time when He would enter a public ministry that would turn the world upside down.

QUESTION TO PONDER

What aspect of the Christmas story impresses you the most?

Day 33

READ: LUKE 3:1–19

John the Baptist's ministry straddles the Old and New Testaments. He is a prophet, calling the people to repent and turn to God and reminiscent of prophets like Elijah. But he also clearly points to Jesus – to the One who will baptise 'with the Holy Spirit and with fire'.

The long introduction in verses 1–2 places John at around AD 29 and is one of the pointers to the dates for Jesus' own ministry, which probably lasted around three and a half years, until His death in AD 33. John's role was to prepare the way for Jesus. We have noted already that Israel was in spiritual exile. Although back in the land, they had largely been a vassal state within the empire of various superpowers and were now under the thumb of the Romans. This humiliation symbolised their spiritual state. They had largely turned their backs on God. There were pious groups such as the Pharisees who believed the route to redemption was zealous following of the Old Testament Law, but this piety created a pride and self-righteousness rather than the humility God required.

So, after a silence of around 400 years, John stands up to call the people to change. It's a change that is to have tangible outcomes. This is not merely a mental agreement that 'I must do better', but a return to the ways of God illustrated here by concern for the poor, honesty in taxation, fairness and contentment. The prophetic element in John's work is seen in his warning that, 'The axe is already at the root of the trees, and every tree that does not produce good fruit will be cut down and thrown into the fire' (v.9). In just forty years God would indeed visit the people of God in judgment, when the Romans destroyed Jerusalem and the Temple in AD 70 – a cataclysmic event for the people of God and one that Jesus Himself would also predict prior to His crucifixion.

John is known as 'the Baptist' because of his practice of baptising those who repented in the River Jordan. This immersion in water was a practice used for non-Jews who wanted to convert.

Some argue that the choice of the River Jordan is symbolic: the people of God first entered Canaan across the Jordan and John calls people here to make a new start.

The end of our narrative anticipates John's sad end. John's fearless preaching includes condemning Herod (son of Herod the Great featured in Matthew 2) for marrying Herodias, the former wife of his brother Philip, in violation of Old Testament Law. Later Herodias's daughter Salome dances before Herod, who offers her a favour in return. Herodias tells her to ask for the head of John the Baptist, which is delivered to her on a plate.

John had many followers, but he was very clear that Jesus was the One whom the people should ultimately follow. If people are ever tempted to applaud us too much, John the Baptist is a great example of someone who was happy to point to the place where worship should be directed.

QUESTION TO PONDER

Is there any Christian whom you are tempted to idolise?

Day 34

READ: LUKE 3:21–38 & 4:1–13

This passage includes the start of Jesus' public ministry. Until this point He had worked as a carpenter in Nazareth in relative obscurity. John the Baptist had been preparing the way by baptising the many thousands who came to him. But one day he looks up and sees Jesus coming forward for baptism. It could have seemed odd, because John's message included the need for repentance. The New Testament makes it clear that Jesus had no sin to confess, and John would have known this. It is in Matthew's Gospel that Jesus explains that He is baptised to 'fulfil all righteousness' (Matthew 3:15). Baptism is a not just a turning away from sin, but also setting one's course towards God. Jesus is making it clear that He is united with John and setting His course to do the will of God.

At Jesus' baptism we see the Father, Son and Holy Spirit involved – first the Father's voice from heaven affirming His Son, using the language of Psalm 2:7 and Isaiah 42:1 describing Jesus as the Son of God, and the Servant of God.

Then we see the Spirit resting upon Jesus like a dove. Jesus is the eternal Son of God but part of His coming to earth meant laying aside the privileges of His sonship. He needed the Holy Spirit's ministry. Luke would later record Peter's speech in Acts 10:38, 'how God anointed Jesus of Nazareth with the Holy Spirit and power, and how he went around doing good and healing all who were under the power of the devil, because God was with him.' If Jesus needed the Holy Spirit's ministry, how much more do we?

It is prior to His public ministry that Jesus receives the affirmation of the Father's love. He had not earned the love through teaching and healing. In the same way our identity is tied up in who we are in Christ, not in what we do for Him, or He does through us.

Luke then reminds us of where Jesus sits in history by providing an abridged genealogy, which most readers skip because it seems dull. But Luke has a purpose in putting it here.

David was promised that there would always be a descendant of his on the throne. Zedekiah was actually the last Davidic king to rule in Judah but Jesus, a descendant of David, was to be the fulfilment of that promise: the eternal King of a different kind of kingdom.

We also see that Jesus is related to all humankind through Adam. He identifies with our humanity, and this reverse chronology means that the last name before the temptations come is that of Adam.

Many believe the forty-day fast in the wilderness is symbolic of Israel who spent forty years in the wilderness. Jesus is a representative of Adam's race and Israel herself. But whereas Israel fails, Jesus succeeds. He responds to the devil by quoting from Deuteronomy, recalling a time when Israel herself had gone through the wilderness and was on the verge of entering the promised land of Canaan. He is tempted in three areas: to question God's care and provision, to engage in false worship and to grab power. Falling for any would have scuppered the divine mission at the very start. Jesus succeeds where Israel failed – the first of many victories over Satan, which culminated in the cross itself.

QUESTION TO PONDER

Do you believe that God says that He is pleased with you?

Day 35

READ: JOHN 3:1–36

Verse 16 of our passage contains the most famous words in the Bible, and the chapter contains a phrase that is sometimes used to sum up Christianity (v.3). But there's much more to note here too.

According to the protocol in that day, the early exchanges in a meeting between two eminent leaders would seek to establish who is in the lead in the conversation. Nicodemus was a Pharisee, a member of a strict religious sect and part of the Jewish ruling council. As such he might have expected to be the senior partner. But Jesus skilfully exposes just how little he really understands in an exchange where He carefully turns the tables. He explains in verse 10 that His talk of flesh and spirit really ought to have been understood by Nicodemus. This is the equivalent of telling a professor of physics that he really should understand the law of gravity! Jesus is probably alluding to Ezekiel 36:25–27, where we see how the Holy Spirit comes to give life to the people. Jesus is outlining to Nicodemus the nature of the revolution that He is bringing to Israel. It will be 'unseen' at one level, but its effects will be powerfully known when the Spirit comes at Pentecost to those who embrace Jesus as Lord. He goes on to anticipate His own death by referencing the way God healed the Israelites in the wilderness when Moses put a bronze snake on a pole (vv.14–15).

The command 'you must be born again' (v.7) has been used by some to identify a particular kind of Christian: 'born again Christians'. In fact 'born again' is the only kind of Christian that is recognised in the New Testament but the phrase is perhaps best translated as 'born from above'. It is the only time the term is used in the New Testament and complements the language used by the other Gospels: Matthew, Mark and Luke who write of 'following Jesus'. The 'born from above' image means God imparts a new kind of life by His Spirit, awakening and quickening the human spirit so that we are brought to repentance and faith in Jesus. It leads us to live a new life in

God, which will involve following Jesus in the ways He taught His disciples to live.

The passage continues with the famous Gospel summary outlining God's commitment to humanity: John 3:16. 'World' refers to all humanity and 'believe' to a solid commitment. This is not saying that whoever merely gives mental assent to the idea that Jesus has died for them will go to heaven, but that everyone who puts their confidence in Jesus will enjoy a new kind of life in the here and now which will extend beyond the earthly life to enjoy presence with God in the new heaven and earth.

The passage does include some sombre words too: verses 18, 19 and 36 remind us that those who refuse to believe are condemned. This condemnation includes the judgment of death but also, in the case of Israel, a judgment at the hands of the Romans, just forty years later, in AD 70.

QUESTIONS TO PONDER

How have you understood the term 'born again' in the past? Do you feel like you understand it better now?

Day 36

READ: LUKE 4:14–44

Many regard this passage as pivotal for an understanding of Jesus' priorities. Luke is outlining the kind of Saviour Jesus was – a prophetic Messiah who took upon Himself the mantle described by Isaiah 40. He is the 'Servant of the Lord' hinted at in that prophecy. But this is not a pleasant return to His home village. Jesus explains that no prophet is welcomed in his home town and highlights the way that Elijah and Elisha were both sent outside Israel. But the people take umbrage and threaten to do away with Him there and then.

It is an extraordinary turn of events. Here are people who could have been on the threshold of seeing extraordinary events in their town/village but who choose to reject the One who could give life, preferring 'offence' to faith.

Jesus underlines what we have hinted at already – He is a man dependent upon the Holy Spirit for His ministry. Although fully God, He lays aside His glory in order to serve as 'one of us' – modelling what it's like for us too to live and move in the power of the Spirit.

Some see this passage as validation for the view that Jesus' primary concern was social justice. Certainly there is that implication. But remember that at that time the poor were regarded as beyond God's blessing. It was thought that they were poor because God had chosen not to bless them, and as outcasts they feared that no one wanted to help them. Jesus is thus challenging conventional wisdom. The 'year of the Lord's favour' was reference to the Year of Jubilee in the Old Testament Law, which stated that every fifty years land should be returned to the original owner and debts written off. We have no proof that this ever happened but the implication of Jesus' words is clear – those in emotional and spiritual debt can have these debts cancelled by Jesus.

If Nazareth was a no-go area, other places loved Jesus. They recognised Him as someone who spoke with authority and backed up His teaching with action. The kingdom of God –

God acting in the world – was being revealed in the miraculous. Something special was happening in Israel that had not been known and seen for hundreds of years, back to the time of the prophets. In the Gospels there are thirty-seven different recorded miracles (some are recorded by more than one writer). These include twenty-three physical healings, with three dead raised. In John's Gospel we are reminded that many more miracles (signs) were seen but not recorded. But none is seen in Nazareth, apart from a few sick being healed (Mark 6:4–5).

QUESTIONS TO PONDER

Have you ever witnessed, or been part of, a miracle?

Why do you think some of us don't see many miracles today?

Day 37

READ: MATTHEW 5:1–48

Known as 'the Sermon on the Mount', Matthew 5 to 7 is one of the best-known and most misunderstood sections in the Gospels. This is the first of five blocks of teaching in Matthew. At the end of the Gospel, Jesus urges His followers to make followers of Him and teach them to obey all that He had commanded.

Jesus was urging His disciples and the crowds that joined them to learn how to live in the kingdom that He lives in. In some respects His teaching stands alongside the Old Testament prophets who called the people of Israel back to God, but, rather than focusing explicitly upon the Law of God (as found in the first five books of the Bible), He looks at living a kind of life that routinely keeps the Law.

This passage opens with a list of people society would have not expected to receive the blessing of God. The Pharisees and teachers of the Law were regarded by many as the arbiters of whom God accepted and whom He didn't, and the poor in spirit, the mourners, the meek etc were not on the list. Jesus is saying that the kingdom of God is available to these people. In our society He might say, 'Blessed are the Aids sufferers, the drug traffickers, those on benefits, the addicts.' Society, and even the Church, may at times shun certain people, but Jesus says that these people are welcome in the kingdom, so that they can learn what it means to follow Him.

Although 'the Sermon' is actually a collection of themes (and was probably never preached as a sermon as such) you can see a progression in thought throughout them. Jesus first underlines the continuity between His ministry and the Old Testament. He 'fulfils' the law for us. We are incapable of fulfilling the law ourselves, and are grateful that He lived the perfect life *for us* and gives us the grace to know inner transformation.

Jesus then turns to topics that are so pivotal within human relationships: anger and lust. These words have been disputed because they seem so impossible – we might manage to refrain from murder and adultery, but anger and lust? His concern with anger is a concern with the sort of anger that leads us to ill treat others. (We feel anger when our will is crossed. Anger itself is not a sin, though it often leads to us commit sin.)

Jesus is saying that by following Him we will be so transformed that sin will lose its attractiveness and goodness will be preferred (through the Spirit's help). We live God's way because we cannot imagine a different way. The Sermon on the Mount is for us today, not left to some future realm. This all amounts to a counter-cultural movement. Followers of Christ are to model a new way that eschews the self-focused competitiveness that pervades many people's lives in favour of a life lived in the full realisation that God provides for us so we do not need to fret and strive. Sound good?

QUESTION TO PONDER

Does this chapter delight you or depress you?

Day 38

READ: LUKE 9:1–51

This is a key and pivotal chapter in Luke's Gospel. That Jesus had twelve disciples is pretty well known, but not everyone knows why. There are clear hints in the Gospels that Jesus deliberately chose twelve to symbolise the twelve tribes of Israel, indicating His connection with the past. But also He was intent on creating a new community. So the choosing of the Twelve was a provocative act. He was also preparing these men to continue the ministry after He had gone. He had a short (probably three-and-a-half-year) ministry and wanted these twelve to be involved in it (see Matthew 28:18f; Acts 1:8). Healing the sick and the casting out of demons would be something that they (and indeed future followers of Jesus) would be doing as a sign of the rule of God breaking into this present world.

The account of the feeding of the 5,000 is a significant miracle, and, as such, is included in all four Gospels. It certainly affects more people immediately than any other, and signifies Jesus' ability to do amazing things. No doubt the disciples recalled the shock they felt when Jesus asked that they 'give them something to eat'! Jesus knew what was possible in the kingdom of God, of course, and wanted to stretch their understanding. It's after they are bemused at the suggestion that the miracle takes place and they learn how their involvement with Him means extraordinary things can happen. They become part of a miracle that shows the people that He is the Great Provider; like God had provided for His ancient people Israel in the desert, this miracle is symbolic of His spiritual provision.

This chapter has a forward momentum in Luke. Jesus predicts His death to the Twelve and people from the Old Testament, Moses and Elijah, join Jesus. (Moses is denied entrance to the promised land when on earth, but makes it there eventually!) We see in the transfiguration that this man has a God-given glory that transcends time and space. We also learn that the pathway of Jesus' followers is also to death (not physical death necessarily, though Church history suggests over half the disciples were martyred) – the death of running life our way. Those that follow need to be single-minded in their devotion.

Though the teaching about discipleship is clear, the disciples themselves are very much a work in progress, and there is evidence of that here as in other parts of the Gospels. All of this can be a comfort to individuals and churches who make similar errors. The disciples, for example, argue about who is the greatest. Their competitive spirit means that they are reluctant to support others who cast out demons, and when a Samaritan village refuses entry to them they are even keen on wiping it out with fire from heaven!

Verse 51 tells us that from this point Jesus is determined to head towards Jerusalem and His cross and resurrection. The rest of the Gospel relates teaching and incidents that have this inevitable destination as the backdrop.

QUESTIONS TO PONDER

Are you at the end of your resources? Have you asked Jesus for help?

In what ways is following Jesus likely to make a difference to your week?

Day 39

READ: LUKE 15:1–32

Maybe as much as fifty per cent of Jesus' teaching was done using parables. Parables are tough to interpret because the rules vary from parable to parable. Sometimes the parable has a number of clear connections between the elements of the parable and real life – such as with the parable of the sower (Matthew 13:3–23). In other occasions a parable may just be making one point, as in the parable of the workers in the vineyard (Matthew 20:1–16).

The last of the three parables in Luke 15 is one of the best known and the least understood. The meaning can be lost by failing to see that the three parables were told because of the kind of company that Jesus was keeping (vv.1–3).

The lost coin and lost sheep are relatively straightforward to decipher. Jesus is drawing a parallel between the joy that a shepherd and a woman have over finding what was lost and the joy felt in heaven over a sinner who repents.

The third parable is more complex. In it we have a story that would have been compelling to the people of the day. The request for the legacy would have been impertinent and the father deemed strange in granting the request. Any son taking the wealth outside of Israel would have been shunned by the community, especially when he had spent it wantonly and ended up feeding pigs (unclean animals within Jewish society). The son expected to be rejected by the family, hence the prepared speech where he asked to be given the job as a servant, not return as a son. But the speech was reconciliation on 'his terms'. In the end he is blown away by his father's extraordinary response. The father is depicted as looking out for his son. He runs to meet him, an action unheard of in that culture. His father doesn't let him finish his speech but welcomes him, not as a servant, but as a son. The son is given symbols of sonship and a party is held as a sign of the father's joy.

The parable is known by some as the Prodigal Son, which emphasises the wayward son's story, but the ending is also significant. The older son also disrespects the father by not joining the party, complaining at the generous treatment of the younger son. And whereas the younger son is clearly reconciled, the parable finishes with a question mark against the older son. The theme of rejoicing, seen with the coin and the sheep parables, is repeated but we do not know whether the older son, who also behaves as someone who is lost, is ever reconciled.

It seems clear that Jesus is cleverly stating that the religious leaders, who had criticised Him, are like the older son. They are apparently within the family but are slaving away, annoyed at the generosity of God (the father) who welcomes the son back. And Jesus thus seems utterly comfortable with the implication that God is the kind of person who runs out to meet us, welcomes us and throws us a party. As such the parable depicts the kind of ministry Jesus exercised. There was always a welcome to those on the fringe of society who had given up on religion. Jesus was quite comfortable keeping company with the immoral and lawless – a decision which of course would drive an increasing wedge between Him and the religious leaders. We can easily adopt the Pharisees' attitude – believing that we slave in the kingdom for God and somehow earn our place, when all the time God accepts us and treats us as sons and daughters, welcomed to be who we are with no strings attached.

QUESTION TO PONDER

Which son do you most identify with – why?

Day 40

READ: JOHN 15:1–27 & 16:1–33

These chapters are part of what is known as 'the Upper Room Discourse' (John 14–17). They take place around the time of the Passover meal that Jesus has with His followers – the meal in which He indicated that bread and wine symbolised His body and blood, which were about to be given up at His crucifixion. They are precious words, representing some of the last teaching that Jesus gave in His earthly life. We have noted already that John's Gospel is very distinct from the other three. Jesus' assertion, 'I am the true vine' is the last of seven 'I am' sayings in the Gospel. It is an extraordinary statement. Israel is known in the Old Testament as 'the vine' and so by using the term 'true vine' Jesus is referring to the way He fulfils the commission given to the people of God, as well as outlining that He is the terminus for all people who would come to know Him. Extraordinary too are Jesus' words stating that the love that God has for Jesus is equal to that which Jesus has for us. Within that glorious context we will bear fruit to the extent that we are linked with Him, a connection that comes and is strengthened by prayer as we receive all needed resources from Him. Effort expended outside of our friendship with Him does nothing. But why would we want to be out of sorts even for a moment – do we have a better alternative?

Such words as 'ask whatever you will and it will be done', may sound like they are straight out of a fairy tale, but they reflect Jesus' desire that we be treated as His friends. He believes the inner heart can be so transformed that we want what God wants and so He is able to grant it. Maybe you are looking for God's will in a matter. You are wise to search the Bible to see what He says and ask wise Christian friends. But, providing you are following His ways, there are occasions when there is no one 'correct route' and He may be asking you what you want to do.

Connectedness will not save us from troubles, which will come to Christ's followers as they came to Him. But His disciples are not to be bereft, as Jesus will be sending His

Spirit to be with them. Jesus says to them, 'It is for your good that I am going away', which implies that it is better for Him to go so that they can be empowered personally by the Holy Spirit. We can have that empowerment for ourselves today.

The Holy Spirit has another key role – that of 'witnessing' alongside believers. Whereas God's people are to speak of what they know of Jesus, the Holy Spirit works within the hearts and lives of people underlining the truth of what they hear. He goes beyond our words, and of course to places and people where we cannot physically go. In prayer we can ask God's Spirit to be at work even today. Where would you like Him to reach?

QUESTION TO PONDER

To what extent to do you know God's daily resources for your life?

Day 41

READ: MARK 11:1–33

All the Gospels give prominence to the last week of Jesus' life. This is not a style of biography you would find today, but follows an ancient style. The 'good news' includes of course understanding the importance of the cross and resurrection, which come at the end of the last week. According to Mark's detailed chronology, Jesus' entry to Jerusalem took place on the Sunday before Easter (29 March if this was AD 33). According to John, Jesus had spent the night before at the house of Lazarus in Bethany. This was to be His base for the week: during the day He and His disciples went to Jerusalem, at night they retreated to Bethany. This chapter charts how Jesus travelled into Jerusalem on a colt, a means of transport that was in stark contrast to the kind of warrior leader that the Jews imagined the 'messiah' would use.

Jesus is welcomed by the people, though their call, 'Hosanna' (meaning literally 'save us'), was calling for a military action. Jesus is subverting expectations all the time. It was certainly a 'grand entrance', over the Mount of Olives, down into the Kidron Valley to the multitudes gathered in tents, or makeshift shelters, in readiness for Passover.

The cursing of the fig tree symbolises Jesus' sadness that the people of Israel had not produced the fruit that God was looking for. He would later in chapter 13 predict a calamity within a generation and, indeed, by AD 70, Jerusalem would be overrun by the Romans and the Temple would be destroyed.

When Jesus enters Jerusalem the next day, He visits the Temple, and becomes angry that the place of worship had become corrupted by commerce. The area designated for Gentiles, and thus symbolising Israel's role as a light to the nations, had become a marketplace, effectively excluding non-Jews. Furthermore, the money-changing practices Jesus despised reflected a monopoly by the Temple, which insisted on a certain form of payment for animals to be sacrificed that increased the wealth of the priestly classes, and in particular the family of Caiaphas. By overturning tables there Jesus is making a direct attack upon the rulers; those He knew would be behind His execution.

Most of the Gospels include sections outlining the antagonism between Jesus and the religious leaders at this time. Jesus was an innocent man, who had lived an extraordinary life of peace and grace. But throughout the Gospels we have noted the mounting hostility from those whom, through His teaching and approach, Jesus undermined in their powerful role as custodians of religion.

The exchange in verses 27 to 33 is typical of the clever and often humorous way that Jesus turned the tables on His adversaries. It meant, however, that their resolve to find a way to kill Him became even stronger. Eventually, thanks in part to Judas, one of the Twelve, they would get their way.

QUESTIONS TO PONDER

Is the place of worship you attend welcoming to outsiders?

Is there anything that you – or your church – do that you think Jesus wouldn't like if He visited today?

Day 42

READ: MATTHEW 26:1–56

The touching story at the start of the chapter is a contrast with much of what follows. A woman who had been healed by Jesus anoints Him with her very best perfume in an act that is clearly prophetic and which the Gospel writers recalled afterwards. The atmosphere is getting darker and evil approaches, but this woman's worship reminds us of what is truly going on and who is ultimately in control.

At this stage in the story the crucifixion of Jesus seems pretty unlikely. Jesus is popular with the people; many have travelled to Jerusalem from Galilee because they had heard His life-changing teaching. Some have even received healing at His hand. The religious authorities are keen to have Him killed but fear an uprising. What they need is someone who can give them His precise location so that they can smuggle Him off and execute Him before the people get wind of it. It is here that Judas' betrayal becomes so significant. They pay him off and he gives the soldiers the precise location in the Garden of Gethsemane, across the Kidron Valley. Betrayal is a heinous act in any country and culture …

It was within this atmosphere that Jesus had His final meal with His disciples. Commentators disagree as to whether it was a Passover meal eaten early, or a meal based on the Passover that Jesus convenes for His own purpose. Certainly there is no mention of lamb, the central dish for a Passover, and, if Jesus sees Himself as 'the lamb' as the apostle Paul would later intimate, He never says so. Jesus uses bread and wine to symbolise His body and blood, which He would shortly offer. Jesus' death would occur just at the time when lambs were slaughtered for the Passover celebration – a clear echo of the first Passover meal in Exodus when Israel was freed from slavery to the Egyptians and understood as such by New Testament writers. The theological meaning of the Communion service (variously named) has been argued about throughout Church history. But in all the Gospels there are just a few lines recounting what Jesus did and said. It was essentially a simple meal with glorious significance for the believer.

If you were going to make up a story about the death of Jesus you would hardly choose to suggest that the main leader of the Early Church, the apostle Peter, had denied Jesus. But this is exactly what happens a little later in the chapter. Peter gets himself into the high priest's courtyard and, fearing for his own life, pretends that he has nothing to do with the Man he has followed for three years. But he is not the only one to leave. By the end of the chapter, all have fled. Symbolically, it is as if all Israel has turned its back on God's anointed. But this turning serves to effect the restoration of that people within the new plans God has for Jew and Gentile to be part of a redeemed people of God.

QUESTIONS TO PONDER

Do you identify with Peter at all?

How do you imagine you would have responded to the servant girl's questions?

Day 43

READ: MATTHEW 26:57–75 & 27:1–66

The death of Jesus stands at the heart of the Christian faith. All believers know that He died for their sins – the perfect sacrifice that sets them free from the penalty of sin, the power of sin and, one day, from the presence of sin. But acknowledging the theological truth does not explain why a man who had been so popular with the people, healing so many, was executed.

The Gospels include occasional references to the way in which the religious authorities despised Jesus and His message. He undermined their own authority by His insistence that they had misunderstood God and the life that He wanted. He also challenged their power base. At this time the priesthood was no longer just a religious matter, but also deeply political. Under Roman rule, the high priest had become a direct Roman appointment and, as such, had to collect taxes and keep law and order.

Jesus is taken to the ruling body, known as the Sanhedrin – a collection of priests, scribes and elders. It is a mock trial convened at night with the verdict pretty well decided. There were seventy-one on the Sanhedrin, but just twenty-three were required to pass sentence. Jesus is charged with planning a terrorist act against the Temple. Caiaphas asks if Jesus is 'the Messiah' (Matthew 26:63–66; Mark 14:61–64) and regards His affirmative answer as proof of His guilt. It was not the claim to be the Messiah which was blasphemous, but the claim to be God.

Israel had no power to execute and so required the Romans to be convinced of Jesus' guilt. (At this time Pilate's position as Roman procurator of Judaea was shaky and so he wanted peace at all costs.) The Jews changed the charge slightly, claiming that Jesus was anti-Rome, and anti-Caeasar, to put further pressure on Pilate. He asked the opinion of the crowds, who answered that they wanted Jesus to be executed. Doubtless the crowds were handpicked by the Temple elite to give the biased reaction – plenty of Jews wanted Jesus to live.

Crucifixion was a death reserved for the lowest classes; for slaves or rebels. It was a shameful death designed to humiliate and terrify. In Jesus' case, the actual hanging on a cross came at the end of a severe beating, which clearly hastened His death. Victims of crucifixion might take several days to die. For Him, the physical death came more quickly, because He had lost too much blood.

There was not much time before sunset and the start of the Sabbath and so Joseph of Arimathea persuaded Pilate to let him have the body of Jesus and give it a decent burial in a family tomb. But, fearing that the disciples might try to pinch the body, Pilate posted a guard, men whose own lives would depend upon guarding the body. Little did they know what would happen next ...

QUESTION TO PONDER

What does Jesus' death mean for you?

Day 44

READ: LUKE 24:1–49

The resurrection of Jesus is a fundamental event to the credibility of Christianity. It proves that His sacrificial death was accepted by His Father and God's plans for the salvation of the world completed. Jesus is now the head of a new humanity, giving life to all who put their confidence in Him. All four Gospels include accounts of the resurrection from different vantage points and Luke tells of the women at the tomb and the two on the road to Emmaus.

Sunday morning would have been the first time the women could approach the body of Jesus after the Sabbath. They clearly had no expectation of finding Jesus alive. If you were fabricating the account, you would be unlikely to have women as the first witnesses. Women's testimonies were only admissible in a Court of Law if no man could be found, and the reaction of the apostles shows that they too had no thought of resurrection.

Those on the road to Emmaus express their massive disappointment that Jesus had not accomplished what they had hoped and are given a seminar in the 'Scriptures' (our Old Testament) as Jesus shows why the Messiah had to suffer and rise. There's much humour here. Note Jesus' understatement, 'What things?' He pretends to go on somewhere else (like He had somewhere to go!) and then disappears when they realise who He is.

Understandably they walk (or jog?) the seven miles back to Jerusalem to share the news, only for Jesus to appear again to give another Old Testament seminar to the Eleven who had assembled in the Upper Room.

So what is Jesus doing here? It was not enough for them just to see Him, but important that they could see how redemptive history had all led up to this point. We have already seen that Jesus coming to earth is inextricably linked with the Old Testament, and this is not just a fanciful notion cooked up by theologians. Jesus Himself testifies to it. Why a 'Bible study' at such a time?

Maybe Jesus is keen that, in the emotion of seeing Him, they have solid biblical evidence to explain His resurrection. This was not hysteria from a group that wanted Him back and were prepared to imagine things, and fabricate stories, but God's programme throughout human history culminating in resurrection. God had raised the dead before, of course, but here was One who rises to life immortal, One who will never die and makes life possible for all who will put their confidence in Him.

And the mission is to continue, as Jesus explains the importance of the message of repentance for the forgiveness of sins being preached to the nations. He also anticipates the coming of the Spirit at Pentecost (recorded in Acts 2). Luke wants us to be in no doubt that as we face our world today, we can face it in the knowledge that the risen Christ can be there with us and in us and for us. We are truly people of the resurrection and no other single event in history can affect our day more than that one.

QUESTION TO PONDER

Are you living in the light of the knowledge you have acquired in this section?

Day 45

READ: MATTHEW 28:1–20

Matthew's account of the resurrection is much shorter and includes the first 'resurrection cover up'. The guards are clearly disturbed by the earthquake that accompanies the resurrection – the tomb had to be open, not to let Jesus out (He demonstrates in other Gospels that this body is not hampered by locked doors), but to show that He has gone. All of this creates a big problem for those who thought they had got rid of Him, and so the guards receive a payoff to claim that the absence of the body is due to the disciples having pinched it!

Our focus here is upon the last words of the book, known as 'The Great Commission'. Jesus is back in Galilee with His eleven disciples, back in the area where He had conducted the bulk of His teaching and many of His miracles. What next? Jesus is risen, but will soon ascend back to heaven. It is now that the last three years' learning from Him is to come into its own, as Jesus explains that His resurrection means that He has all authority. In view of this, the disciples' job is to make more followers of Him. He won't be there in person anymore, but His Spirit will be wherever they go (and tradition suggests they would go to all four points of the compass with the good news).

The Church's general failure to grasp the teaching of Jesus on this point means we must underline what Jesus is looking for.

We are told to 'make' Christ followers (not converts) from all ethnic groups. This is a fulfilment of God's purposes expressed in the call of Abraham that all nations of the world would one day be blessed. The making of Christ followers would be through two things: immersing them in the Trinitarian life of God, and teaching them to obey Jesus' teaching. This is more than getting converts wet and saying 'in the name of the Father, Son and Holy Spirit' over them, but helping them understand what it means for God to be leading and empowering their lives. Teaching them to obey Jesus' teaching will take a little longer, of course, and we know that Matthew has arranged his Gospel with five blocks of teaching that could ideally form the curriculum, starting with the so-called Sermon on the Mount in chapters 5 to 7. Obedience to Jesus is to be the chief dimension of being a follower. He calls the shots from now on. Whatever Christianity would become, this should be at its heart, a wholehearted commitment to learning how to obey what Jesus said. So mental agreement about Jesus is but a start. Some will claim to be Christian without having the first idea about obeying Jesus' teaching.

The order of Jesus' words is doubtless significant. You try obeying the teaching without the Trinitarian life of God within you! Many have tried and wound up frustrated, depressed and despairing. It is too hard. But thankfully our hearts can be so transformed that we become the kind of people who naturally want to do what He requires, and so become like Christ to a world that doesn't know Him.

QUESTION TO PONDER

Are there ways your church could better teach people how to follow Jesus?

Day 46

READ: ACTS 1:1–26 & 2:1–47

The risen Jesus had been teaching the apostles on and off for forty days, and told them that it was imperative that they stay in Jerusalem to await the gift of the Holy Spirit – the same Spirit who had empowered His own ministry since His baptism and whom He had spoken of in the Upper Room meeting shortly before His death.

It would be the disciples' job to be witnesses to His life and spread news of Him to the ends of the earth. So they waited in Jerusalem, and it is on the Day of Pentecost that Jesus' promise is fulfilled. Pentecost is celebrated seven weeks (fifty days) after Easter Sunday and it was normal for Jews from around the world to gather for the annual celebration. It was the time of the first fruits, similar to Harvest Thanksgiving services celebrated in many churches today.

It is not clear whether the Spirit comes to just the twelve apostles (now including Matthias, who replaced Judas) or more. In 1:15 there is mention of 120 believers, but chapter 2:1, in which Pentecost starts, comes directly after mention of the Twelve. The gift of the Spirit is signified by tongues of fire and an ability to declare the wonders of God in languages not previously learned – known as the gift of tongues. Jesus' desire that the apostles would make disciples of all nations is about to become true, even before they had left the capital! Maybe the number of nations listed suggests there were more than twelve who received the gift, unless of course the apostles were each enabled to speak more than one language.

The great commotion caused by the apostles soon creates a crowd and Peter has an opportunity to explain what is going on by quoting from the Old Testament. He explains that this is the fulfilment of Joel's prophecy of the coming of the Holy Spirit (Joel 2:28–29). This is also connected with the resurrection of Jesus just a few short months before, which had also been promised in 2 Samuel 7:12–13. In other words, God's programme of restoration is on track and now the good news of Jesus can be enjoyed by all peoples ('those who are far off'). He mentions too that the Jews had crucified Jesus and that, though this was part of God's purposes, they were still culpable. It was a stirring message and shook many of the hearers. They responded as Peter suggested, in repentance and baptism, with 3,000 added to the Church that day.

The passage is a wonderful description of the birth of the Church. Sadly many have misunderstood its role, believing it to be the only way the Holy Spirit comes to people today, when Acts alone includes many other descriptions of the Spirit's gift that are different from this. What is clear is that *all* need that empowering of the Spirit for witness. Here are men who heard the wonderful teaching of Jesus and witnessed and participated in His miracles, and yet they needed the gift of the Spirit to have the boldness and courage to take the message worldwide and continue the fulfilment of God's desire that the ends of the earth would hear the news of His saving love. We are commissioned to continue spreading this message. If they needed the Spirit you and I do, too.

QUESTION TO PONDER

Do you sense God's empowerment to share the good news of Jesus with others?

Day 47

READ: ACTS 10:1–48

In Acts 1 the risen Jesus had told His followers that when the Holy Spirit came upon them, they would be His witnesses in Jerusalem, Judaea, Samaria and the ends of the earth, a complementary statement to the Great Commission in Matthew 28:18. For the gospel of Jesus to be taken to the Gentiles the apostles had to overcome their own prejudice. There were strict laws in the Old Testament governing who you could and couldn't eat with and what you could and couldn't eat. Despite being told that they were to make disciples of all nations, and despite God-fearing Jews from many nations having received the Spirit in Acts 2, it took a while for 'the shekel to drop' and Peter had to be jolted into action by a vision asking him to eat foods that were previously embargoed. He later explains in his message that he now understands that 'God does not show favouritism but accepts men from every nation who fear him and do what is right' (v.34).

Caesarea was a significant port then, the place where the Roman Governor, Pontius Pilate, had his residence. It is here that Cornelius, a Roman centurion, has a vision to send for Peter. Peter has a vision further south at Joppa, and is told by the Spirit to go with the men sent to fetch him.

Quite clearly God has to intervene for these people to hear the good news. Some have even subtitled the book of Acts 'The Acts of the Holy Spirit'. He chooses a man who was already God fearing and active with what faith he had. But whereas at Pentecost the Spirit came as they were praying, this time the Holy Spirit falls on those listening to Peter preach – and even before he reaches the punch line! The hearers are given the same gift of tongues that had been given in Acts 2. God was making it crystal clear to a sceptical apostle that He was intending to fulfil His promise to bless all nations of the earth.

Incidentally, this is one of four occasions when the Holy Spirit comes to distinct groups in the New Testament.

The others are in Acts 2 to those gathered in Jerusalem; in Acts 8 to Samaritan believers, and in Acts 19, to those who had been disciples of John the Baptist.

The church leaders in Jerusalem, who had oversight of mission at this time, were just as prejudiced as Peter and so he would have had to explain to them what had happened. The gift of tongues would have been a pivotal part of the explanation as it demonstrated a connection between the gift given at Pentecost in Acts 2 and this same gift now given to Gentiles, something they were not expecting. Tongues is not always a necessary element of receiving the Spirit, and today most churches believe that the Spirit is given as someone comes to faith in Jesus. Tongues may or may not be a gift that the new believer receives. But this vital moment in the book of Acts is of massive significance for all non-Jews. God is showing that He is welcoming all nations to be His people. The promise to Abraham that all nations of the world would be blessed is coming wonderfully true.

QUESTION TO PONDER

Have there been times when God has had to shake you out of a rut in a way that seemed unusual at the time?

Day 48

READ: ACTS 15:1–35

This passage, known as 'The Council of Jerusalem', is a major development in the life of the Church. They were struggling to understand what needed to happen for the Gentiles to be embraced by Jewish Christians as part of the people of God. Circumcision of males was a sign of the covenant (agreement) that God had made with Abraham, and had been practised by Jews ever since. Some believers assumed it must be, therefore, a necessary rite for these new Gentiles. This issue was one that Paul had to face head on in his ministry, and is explored in more detail in some of his letters, notably Galatians.

Paul has been a central figure in Acts since his conversion in Acts 9. This zealous Pharisee received a vision of the risen Jesus as he was travelling to persecute Christians and, after time reflecting on what this meant to his understanding of the Old Testament, had become a key missionary for the growing Church. The church in Antioch, Syria had sent Paul and Barnabas off on their first missionary journey. Paul's strategy was to visit and teach in the synagogues that were located in the major towns and cities, and spread to preaching to Gentiles if and when the Jews refused to listen. The leaders in Jerusalem were very much the mother church attempting to make sense of the expansion of the gospel message across the Roman world.

The text talks of a 'sharp dispute' (v.2) between the believers from Judea and Paul and Barnabas, and we can be sure that the issue was a pivotal one for the Church at this time. Paul and Barnabas felt it necessary to see the Jerusalem leaders and explain their views, hoping to reach unity over the matter. Verse 5 suggests that some took the view that believers needed to 'keep the law' as well as be circumcised.

Two arguments determine the outcome of the Council. The first is the experience of the apostle Peter. His visit to Caesarea opened his eyes to what God was doing among the Gentiles. And he explains that 'the yoke of the law' is not something that Jews have been able to bear – so why place such a yoke upon Gentiles? James, the half brother of Jesus, then presents the argument that Amos 9:11–12 had prophesied that Gentiles would be included within the people of God, and so what Peter had observed was part of God's intentions from centuries before. The upshot of the discussions is that they should not insist that Gentiles be circumcised or keep the Law of Moses, but that they should give them some advice which would ensure that Jewish-Gentile relations remained strong. This was all included in a letter that was sent back to Antioch with respected men.

This respectful dialogue is seen by many as a model for how to overcome controversy. First we need to communicate what is going on, rather than bad mouthing those we perceive to be the opposition. We need to examine experience and Scripture together: both have a part to play, and we need to mutually agree outcomes that will further the cause of the gospel and the unity of the Body. If only the Church throughout history had followed this biblical model!

QUESTIONS TO PONDER

How have you handled disagreements with other believers in the past? Has today's passage taught you anything new about how to handle such difficulties?

Day 49

READ: ROMANS 8:1–39

Romans is seen by many as the apostle Paul's finest explanation of the gospel. This chapter comes at the end of a long line of argument within the epistle (letter) as Paul clarifies his understanding of how faith in Jesus, under the new covenant, works in the light of what God was doing under the old covenant with Israel. He will go on in chapters 9 to 11 to outline how we are to understand God's ongoing work with the people of Israel, and in chapter 14 to deal with some of the problems in the church of Rome between those with a Jewish background and those from a Gentile background.

This chapter explores the glories of the life in the Spirit that we are promised. We are not under condemnation if we are in Christ! The Law of God had a good and important role, but it could not reconcile us to God. Christ has done this in His death and resurrection, and the Spirit works out the truth of our salvation in us as we cooperate with Him.

We have noted before that we need to put to death whatever displeases God: 'For if you live according to the sinful nature, you will die; but if by the Spirit you put to death the misdeeds of the body, you will live ...' (v.13).

Paul is also keen to emphasise a theme that occurs elsewhere in his letters. Using the image of the common legal practice of adopting a male heir into a Roman household, Paul explains that Christians are adopted into God's family and will inherit all that God has for Christ. Whatever your economic inheritance, you have unfathomable riches reserved in an account in heaven with your name on it.

Paul then anticipates those who think that this is all very well, but what about life in the real world? He looks at suffering alongside these riches and concludes that, in the overlap of living by the Spirit in this world, some form of suffering is inevitable. He takes us back to the creation of the world. The entrance of sin into the world led to God's cursing of the land. God's redemptive plan is that creation itself will end its pain when those who are redeemed enter into the new heaven and earth. In the meantime, as those made for glory, we suffer the pain of not yet being where we long to be. This includes the weakness we experience in prayer. We can't form the words to express what we feel. Thankfully Paul assures us that the Spirit interprets our own groans for us (vv.23,26). Indeed in a wonderful way, even in suffering, God is at work in those who are His people, so that they become more Christlike as they live through pain. Although many things may masquerade as coming between us and our position in Christ, nothing actually can. These believers, and us 2,000 years later, are as safe in Christ as we can be, whatever the obstacles.

QUESTIONS TO PONDER

Have you ever thought that you had been separated from the love of Christ? What gave you the confidence to believe again that He loved you?

Day 50

READ: 1 CORINTHIANS 12:1–31 & 13:1–13

The church in Corinth was one that had grown through Paul's preaching. In Acts 18:9–11 the Lord appeared to Paul in a vision, assuring him that many would come to faith in that city and that he was not to fear. He was to speak out boldly, rather than to hold back for fear of trouble. As a result, Paul extended his ministry in Corinth staying a total of eighteen months, which was an unusually long time for the apostle.

Corinth was a cosmopolitan city on a trade route. Luxuries from all over the world were available, and the vices of the world were also to be found. The church's immaturity had led to a series of letters from Paul, including what we know as 1 and 2 Corinthians. Parts of the letters seem to be Paul's answers to questions they had raised, and it may be that 'spiritual gifts' was one of them. Paul covers spiritual gifts here and in Romans 12 and Ephesians 4. A number of things are clear: all true believers in Jesus have the Holy Spirit (12:13) and all are given spiritual gifts for the benefit of the Body of Christ. There is no suggestion that the list of gifts here, or elsewhere, is exhaustive (eighteen are listed in Paul's letters). Some are more obviously supernatural (such as working miracles of healing and tongues) but Paul is keen to stress that each is valuable. The cartoon-like image of body parts speaking to each other reminds us that just as all body parts matter, all the gifts have the same value to God. It was never intended that only those 'ordained' should minister. All have ministries useful to the Body. Chapter 12 and chapter 14 reflect a style of service that leaves room for those gathered to exercise the speaking gift they have been given. The questions at the end of chapter 12 suggest, of course, that we all need one another because no one has all the gifts.

Chapter 13 is often read separately from its context as a beautiful celebration of love, usually at wedding ceremonies. In fact, Paul wrote on spiritual gifts from chapters 12 to 14 and they should be viewed as a whole as the chapter divisions were added later. Christian character is also a fruit of the Spirit's work and here Paul is saying that someone might exercise spiritual gifts (in this case tongues, prophecy, faith and giving) but if they don't do so out of love they completely miss the point. Paul spells out what love is – 'the more excellent way' – to a church that lauded the spectacular but had missed what God was seeking to develop in their characters. Jesus of course exemplified every virtue perfectly and His name could replace love throughout the chapter. And whereas many of the gifts will not be needed in the hereafter, love will be the glorious atmosphere of heaven. So, whatever gifts you have, do you have love too? – for yourself – as Christ's Beloved?

QUESTIONS TO PONDER

In what ways do you serve the Body of believers where you worship? Self-care & encouragement of others + seeking wisdom & fellowship to increase in understanding & intimacy with our Father

How loving are you in your day-to-day life, not just in church?

not loving enough because I rely on my own limited capacity & imagination rather than totally relying on God

Day 51

READ: GALATIANS 5:1–26

In Galatians Paul is especially concerned with those who were arguing that followers of Jesus needed to be circumcised to be saved, an issue noted in our look at Acts 15. This custom, strange to modern eyes, had been a sign of the covenant God made with Abraham, regarded as the great forefather of Judaism. Paul explains that Abraham was justified by faith before he was circumcised and so he is the 'father' of all who believe – Gentiles included. He was revealing that God looks at our faith, not whether we keep His laws. Paul's passion for his point of view resonates throughout the letter; you can still sense a preacher's instinct as he urges his readers to walk in the Spirit at the start of this chapter.

Paul contrasts walking by the Spirit with the two evils of legalism and licence. Legalism argues that you are saved by keeping the law, in particular circumcision; licence argues that you can live as you like, because Jesus had paid the price for your sin. His language is firm: 'You who are trying to be justified by the law have been alienated from Christ; you have fallen away from grace' (v.4). Similarly, those who are licentious 'will not inherit the kingdom of God' (v.21).

The better way is the way of the Spirit, which leads to the character of Jesus being reproduced in us. Nine characteristics are listed for us in verses 22 and 23. The fruit imagery signifies the way in which the believer who is connected to Christ (remember the image of the vine in John 15) naturally produces fruit. We need to utilise the means of grace that He gives: notably obeying His Word, praying, spending time with other Christians, worshipping God etc. We do not, indeed we cannot, force ourselves to be godly. It is true that we need to make an effort: at times we may find spiritual disciplines a struggle, but this is not the effort of people frightened of whether they will make the grade but the joyful response of hearts gripped by God's love and kindness towards us.

Hence, for Paul, the Holy Spirit's ministry is vital for all the fledgling churches that had developed. His battle with legalists would dog him throughout his ministry. It is an issue that is not absent today, as well-meaning church leaders seek to add particular patterns of living to the freedom we enjoy in Christ. It killed true Christianity in Paul's day and it will do the same for us today if we let it.

QUESTION TO PONDER

Are you enjoying the freedom of life in the Spirit?

Day 52

READ: EPHESIANS 1:1–23

The Ephesian epistle is believed to be one of the finest expositions of Paul's theology. The Ephesian church stood at the heart of pagan religion in a city revered for its occult practices, but the letter is not due to any particular issue or heresy – at least so it would seem.

This opening chapter, which outlines God's purposes for His people, has perplexed many. Christians have interpreted it in two ways: some believe that God selects those who are going to be Christians; others argue that God simply foreknows what people will decide. But the passage does not actually mention whether God selects or not, merely that just as God elects Israel in the Old Testament, so He has decided that all who come to Christ are included in many things, chiefly God's plan to make people holy in His sight. (Predestination here refers to the state of those in Christ, not to whether one person is selected or not.) So however you understand this passage, if you are a believer in Jesus, you can rejoice that God has purposes for you. Specifically you have been brought back to God by the blood of Jesus, your sins are forgiven and you have an awareness of the purposes of God in the world now. He has made you a son too, signifying that you will inherit all that the Father has given to His own Son. You have also been given the Holy Spirit as a down payment of all that God wants to give you one day. Paul wants his readers to be absolutely sure of who they are. Their inclusion in Christ is a wonderful gift according to His love and kindness to them.

Paul prays for the believers that they might truly know God Himself experientially, which includes knowing the same power that raised Jesus from the dead (vv.19–20). How much power do we need in the Christian life? We have *all* we need in Christ.

Paul writes of God bringing all things under Christ one day (v.10), knowing that all things are under His authority (vv.22–23). There is nothing more significant happening in the world today than that which is part of God's redeeming purpose for this planet. Somehow He is always at work, even when evil seems to be having the upper hand.

The passage should lead to rejoicing but not passivity. There's a battle on for us to live in the good of what Paul tells us is true of us and the Christians around us. So, in view of this, is it a surprise that Paul calls upon the Ephesians, and us, to praise Him?

Covid
Famine
Drought
Trafficking
Illness
Addictions
Abuse

QUESTION TO PONDER
Which part of the passage do you need to meditate on further, or perhaps even memorise?

Day 53

READ: COLOSSIANS 3:1–17

Paul's epistles are rich with exhortations to godly living, and this passage from Colossians sums up the kind of teaching you will find elsewhere in his letters. But they are easily misunderstood. If you miss the process that Paul teaches, you can end up finding Christianity twice as hard as the laws in the Old Testament, and many timid and sensitive souls have become burdened as a result.

It's important to spot that the passage begins with who we are in Christ, who is seated in the heavenly realms. We look forward to the day when Christ comes back to wind things up, but, in the meantime, there is work to be done. There are things that are part of us 'naturally' which need to die (vv.5–9). The implication is that these habits and behaviours are not to be tolerated but are to be replaced with virtues. As he exhorts good behaviour, Paul reminds the Colossians who they are again: 'God's chosen people, holy and dearly loved' (v.12) before describing the kind of life that such people will live.

Interestingly Paul does not explore 'how' we put things to death and clothe ourselves with these virtues. Doubtless he assumes the people are already engaging in the spiritual disciplines that were part of Early Church life, such as Bible reading, prayer, fasting, worship, solitude and silence. These 'means of grace' enable us to position ourselves so that God can do within and for us what we cannot do for ourselves.

It is worth remembering that Paul does not give a timeframe here, and in other letters was quick to explain that he had not attained perfection himself. But this does not mean that we should tolerate sin, or be flippant about virtue.

At the very end of the passage we are told that God's intention is that all of life be lived drawing on His energy. 'In the name of the Lord Jesus' (v.17), means living through His resources and for His glory. Anything we do, providing it is not sinful, can be done in God's power: whether at school or college, in daily employment or at home. Everything we do matters to God. There is no sacred/secular divide in Paul's writings: we are all to be in full-time Christian service: the taxi, hair salon, factory, shed or office may not have religious symbolism, but all can be places of worship.

QUESTIONS TO PONDER

What are you doing today? Will you do it in the name of Jesus?

Day 54

READ: 2 TIMOTHY 3:1–17 & 4:1–8

Paul's letters to Timothy and Titus have been widely called the 'Pastoral Epistles' and, though later scholarship has resisted that label, there's no doubt that church leaders down the ages have found much within them to shape their priorities. Widely believed to be Paul's last letter, 2 Timothy is Paul's advice to his young friend whom he had mentored and sent to help the church at Ephesus. The letter includes his personal concern for his young friend and hints that Paul may be put to death soon.

The gloomy beginning to this section describes society throughout the ages and across the world. The 'last days' do not refer to a period immediately before Christ's return but to the time between Christ's first and second coming. Paul insists that those who behave in certain ways are to be shunned, lest they contaminate the Church. He is not suggesting no contact, after all, Paul elsewhere urges us to communicate with those who don't know God (1 Corinthians 9). His point is that inappropriate connection might lead the believers astray. He warns too, against those who were teaching heresy. Even at a time when the Christians were working out how to understand Jesus in the light of the Old Testament, they could still discern truth from error.

Timothy is encouraged here to emulate Paul's lifestyle. It is a courageous and godly man who would urge others to 'do as I do' – but Paul could do just that and exhorts us all to be the kind of people who model a Christlike walk. He also exhorts Timothy to focus upon the Scriptures, which he had been brought up to love. They are God breathed and therefore play a vital role in his growth as a man of God. Verse 16 reminds us that God has literally 'breathed out' His Word. He has used the minds and personalities of the authors of Scripture, including those who have edited and compiled the writings and sayings of others, to form what we know as the Old Testament. These are the writings that were known and enjoyed by Jesus, the apostles and those who would come to faith in Christ, and were used alongside the circulating apostolic letters and later Gospels.

It's no surprise that Paul should return to the central importance of preaching the Word of God. This was to characterise Timothy's ministry in Ephesus. There will always be those who want a more palatable message, but Paul was reminding him to stay calm and level headed in such circumstances and press on with revealing what God says, not what he or they want him to say. There is a sense of Paul passing on the baton to his young friend here, aware that the time for his own departure is near (4:6). He faces the prospect confident that he will receive a rich welcome into God's presence.

QUESTIONS TO PONDER

How important is the Bible to you?

Do you face death with the same confidence as Paul?

Day 55

READ: HEBREWS 11:1–40

Being a Christian within the Roman Empire was like being a second-class citizen. The Romans allowed the Jews to practise their religion but had not extended this courtesy to Christianity. The letter to the Hebrews hints at some of the sufferings and injustices suffered by those who had converted from Judaism to Christianity. It was tempting for some to side step the hard times by returning to Judaism. The letter to the Hebrews was written to assure them that Christianity is the true heir to the promises of God and that a return to Judaism would be catastrophic.

The book was possibly based on a sermon and aims to demonstrate the superiority of life under the new covenant that Jesus brought in. In chapter 11 the unknown author shows how the purposes of God have remained unchanged even though the Old Testament saints did not have the clarity of vision of the future hope that we have in Christ.

The author includes his heroes of the faith, moving from creation to Abraham, with a few verses of explanation and then from Abraham to Rahab, with brief mentions of others, just as if he is preaching and has to summarise the other names that he could have mentioned.

The actions taken 'by faith' are various. They include worship offering, death, building an ark, moving to a foreign country, having a baby at an old age, offering a child back to God, blessing offspring, making arrangements for final burial, hiding a child, siding with God's downtrodden people, fleeing Egyptians, marching around enemy city walls, harbouring spies, conquering kingdoms, administering justice, shutting the mouths of lions and quenching the fury of the flames. The writer concludes the list by reflecting on those who suffered for their faith.

The author unites these great heroes of the faith to us by explaining that none of them actually received what they had been promised. God had planned something better for them so that 'only together with us would they be made perfect' (v.40).

We have noted many times that God's purposes in Scripture can be best understood in retrospect. Looking back from the time of the gospel we can see what God was doing all along. We have the whole Scripture and can see God's faithfulness throughout time to all His people, but these heroes had far less to go on than us. Abraham could not consult a Bible dictionary when he heard the first call to leave home.

The author goes on in chapter 12 to urge us to continue giving ourselves to the glorious task of making God's glory known in the world. We call the people in these chapters 'heroes of the faith'. But we can be heroes too, if we, by faith, are prepared to act in equivalent ways in our own situation. Be assured that God is with you always, and that His purposes may well blow your mind. What a great incentive to trust Him.

QUESTION TO PONDER

What 'by faith' action is God calling you to take?

Day 56

READ: JAMES 2:14–25 & 3:1–18

The book of James has been called 'the Proverbs of the New Testament' as its style is less a reasoned argument and more a series of pithy sayings about new life in Christ. Its author is probably the half brother of Jesus, who came to believe in Him after the resurrection and is described by Paul as one of the pillars of the Jerusalem church. The book is addressed to the Jewish believers who were scattered across the Roman world.

The letter is perceived as controversial because some believe it contradicts the teaching of the apostle Paul. Paul argues for 'justification by faith'. James seems to argue for justification by works (v.18) leading some to claim that they are preaching a different message and that there cannot, therefore, be a unified message in the New Testament.

The key to this conundrum comes in verse 14. James is speaking about those who 'claim' to have faith but have no deeds to accompany such faith. The apostle Paul preached justification by faith, but he too expected appropriate deeds to accompany such a faith. Throughout his epistles Paul tells his readers that there is a way of living that will flow naturally from justification. So true faith is not merely intellectual assent, but an active faith that leads to character change and a life of good deeds, as illustrated by Abraham and Rahab. So James is not preaching a different message at all, merely clarifying the kind of saving faith that God requires.

Having considered those who claim to have faith, James moves on to look at the importance of speech itself, reminding readers that those who teach have to reach a high standard, not least because speaking many words leads to many opportunities for mistakes. The tongue can do a lot of damage. Just as a rudder controls a ship, or a spark ignites a forest fire, what we say has great ramifications for good or ill. The end of this section is reminiscent of Jesus, who had spoken about how our character determines the kind of fruit we produce (Matthew 7:18), and here James shows that our speech flows from what is inside us.

In 3:13, James returns to his earlier theme. If people want to claim that they are wise, then he wanted to see good living and not the envy and selfish ambition that can characterise gatherings that claim to be Christian but are actually, according to James, 'demonic'. We can know that God is truly involved in people's lives when we see the kind of wisdom they produce: peace-loving, considerate, submissive, full of mercy and good fruit, impartial and sincere. Such fruit has parallels with the apostle Paul's own teaching about the kind of character that the Spirit imparts. This is another reason to believe that, contrary to what some suggest, they are both firmly on the same page.

QUESTIONS TO PONDER

Could your neighbourhood, village, town, city and nation use the kind of wisdom that James describes right now?

How tame is your tongue?

Day 57

READ: 1 PETER 1:1–25 & 2:1–10

After disappearing from the scene after the first half of the book of Acts, little is known of the apostle Peter. It would seem he had an ongoing ministry to reach and equip those from a Jewish background, and was, according to Church tradition, finally martyred in Rome. 'God's elect' (vv.1–2), may refer to Jews, God's chosen people from the time of Abraham, or it may refer to *all* who are now part of God's people, whether Jew or Gentile. The tone of the letter tells us that the people to whom Peter was writing were suffering persecution for their faith and he was keen to remind them of the wonderful faith they needed to persevere in. The hymn of praise in chapter 1 is reminiscent of Paul (see Ephesians 1), as Peter rehearses the work of God in bringing us to new life through the resurrection of Jesus. He reminds his readers that their trials are enabling their faith to grow and be proved genuine and that their hearts can be filled with joy even alongside the trials they are enduring.

He reminds them that prophets spoke of the coming Messiah without knowing a great deal about what they were predicting, but aware that one day a people would come who would know and love the One they spoke about. In view of this the believers needed to think clearly and shun evil. Leviticus 19:2 commands God's people to be holy and this is no less the case here under the new covenant, which brought the death of Jesus, a death which God had planned even before the world had been created (vv.17–21). The connections between the events of Jesus' life, death and resurrection have been brought home to the readers through God's Word (vv.23–25). This Word needs to be at the heart of the people's spiritual growth too (2:1–3).

In chapter 2 Peter uses language that makes it clear that the apostles see the Church, made up of Jewish believers and Gentiles, as 'God's chosen people'. The language formerly used just of God's ancient people is now imported to refer to us today. We are 'living stones ... being built into a spiritual house to be a holy priesthood, offering spiritual sacrifices acceptable to God through Jesus Christ' (2:5). We are also 'a chosen people, a royal priesthood, a holy nation' (2:9). All this is because of Jesus. Peter quotes Isaiah 28:16 here and applies the Messianic stone reference to Jesus, stating that He is the cornerstone that the rest of the building would be built onto.

Peter explains that God is doing a new and special thing, but in continuity with His ancient people, fulfilling that promise in Abraham that all peoples in the world would be blessed through him. God's restoration of all things remains on track and Peter is encouraging these persecuted believers by reminding them of this glorious truth. Whatever you are facing today, you can do so as one who is also God's special possession.

QUESTION TO PONDER

Are you able to praise God the way Peter does, even in the midst of difficulties?

Day 58

READ: 1 JOHN 1:1–10 & 2:1–6

The apostle John was one of the few of Jesus' disciples who was not martyred for his faith. His three letters are believed to be written much later than others in the New Testament. By this point John had had a long time to reflect upon his extraordinary three years in the physical presence of Jesus. The content of 1 John suggests that he is combating a heresy that had developed that was undermining the faith of the believers, possibly in and around Ephesus where John was probably based. False teachers had split the church community and it is possible that their heresy included a belief that Jesus was not fully human. Hence John's opening assertion that he had witnessed Jesus' humanity first hand.

Throughout the letter John is concerned that his readers imitate God. His first mention of the character of God is that He is light, and in Him there is no darkness at all. Light is a metaphor of purity – the psalmist writes of God being clothed in garments of light (Psalm 104:2). He speaks also of God's revelation as being a 'lamp to my feet and a light for my path' (Psalm 119:105). God's character is the standard for all that is good and right in the world. John then goes on to explore the tension we find as believers. We are encouraged to walk in the light with others, avoiding and shunning the sin that prevents close fellowship with other believers. Yet at the same time we acknowledge that we are sinners and therefore will need to confess sin to receive forgiveness and cleansing from God. To be quite sure his readers understand this John underlines it at the start of chapter 2. Jesus is the One who goes into the courts of heaven and pleads on our behalf. Jesus' death provided the sacrifice that we need – and the rest of the world needs.

John is keen to give his readers ways in which they can be sure of their faith. Here he tells them that following Jesus' commands is a sure sign that God is at work within them. Furthermore, 'Whoever claims to be in him must walk as Jesus did' (2:6). This is one of a number of statements in the epistle that can make readers swallow hard. But we have already seen that the New Testament encourages and expects that those who follow Christ will become like Him. If we find this 'impossible' then we are correct in our assessment. We can't do it in our own strength, but need God by His Spirit to change us from the inside out so that we start to think, feel and act as Jesus would. It may seem a tall order, but John, who had seen Him with his own eyes, had experienced this for himself and believed that you and I can too.

QUESTION TO PONDER

When you think of 'walking like Jesus did', what comes to mind?

Day 59

READ: REVELATION 1:1–20

Interpreting the book of Revelation is a challenging business, and some have come unstuck because they are unfamiliar with the literary style. The author employs an ancient style known as apocalyptic, which is highly symbolic. This style was employed on a few occasions in the Old Testament, notably in the second half of Daniel, parts of Ezekiel and the second half of Zechariah. It was used to describe momentous events but also to shield the meaning from those persecuting God's people. This style was used in Revelation to bolster the faith of the readers when they may have been tempted to give up. The early verses remind us that John, perhaps the apostle, was given the vision of Revelation when incarcerated on the island of Patmos as a punishment for preaching the gospel. We don't know what his exact crime was, but commentators speculate that the cult of emperor worship heavily penalised Christians who were not prepared to toe the line.

Many also struggle to interpret the book because they fail to realise that it is rooted in the Old Testament. It contains more than 500 allusions to the Old Testament, and 278 of the 404 verses in Revelation (that is almost seventy per cent) make some reference to the Old Testament. Hence the original readers, many converts from Judaism, would have instantly spotted what John was saying. Unfortunately popular modern-day authors, not so well versed in the Old Testament, have made outrageous claims, unaware of the errors they have made.

This first chapter assures us that the Jesus who lived, died and rose again is returning to earth to bring salvation and judgment and that He continues to be interested and concerned about those who witness for Him. John goes on to depict the risen Jesus' words to seven churches in the Roman province of Asia, which is the western part of modern-day Turkey (see chapters 2 and 3).

John's vision of Jesus picks up on the Old Testament background. He is a priestly figure, with authority, strength and majesty echoing the son of man figure in Daniel 7:13–14.

John was clearly shocked to see this vision: 'I fell at his feet as though dead' (v.17). Jesus reassured him, reminding him of His victory over death and commanding him to write what he saw – of the now and what's yet to come. The book of Revelation reminds readers that whoever may seem to have the upper hand in the short term, Jesus has all authority and will vindicate His own and win the day. While the book does indeed relate to the end times, when interpreting Revelation it is worth remembering that the book had a primary meaning for the readers of the day.

This chapter also includes a reminder that we are to be what Israel largely failed to be, 'a kingdom and priests to serve his God and Father' (v.6). God's aim that human beings should bear His image and spread the rule and reign of God throughout the earth remains. Well might John say, 'to him be glory and power for ever!' This book will go on to show how God's restoration project for the world will come to glorious completion.

Whatever comes your way, whatever your job title or role in life, God sees you as one of His priests. How does that sound?

QUESTION TO PONDER

Are you ready for the priestly role God has for you?

Day 60

READ: REVELATION 21:1–27 & 22:1–21

Ask most Christians where they are going when they die and the answer would be 'Heaven, of course'. It is a glorious prospect for the believer, and indeed the hope of many non-believers who mistakenly believe all will go well when they die.

In fact the ultimate destination for us is a new heaven and new earth. We talk of 'going to heaven' when we die, meaning that our souls will go into the presence of Christ. But we await the events of Revelation 21 and 22, when God Himself will come to dwell on earth, and will renew all things. We are not destined for a disembodied existence floating off somewhere, as some suggest, but will enjoy renewed bodies fit for purpose in a new world that will have some similarity to what we enjoy now. However, there will be no more death, crying or pain. God will dwell with us, the curse will be over and we will reign with Him.

In chapter 21 John has a vision of Jerusalem coming down from heaven. The city is historically the place where God dwelt in the Temple. The dimensions of the city are beyond what we can imagine: 12,000 stadia high, wide and long (12,000 stadia translates to 1,500 miles). Twelve is the number of completeness and it would seem likely that the figures merely symbolise an immense size that covers the earth and reaches the clouds within which God's protective presence is known and felt. This city is a place of order and beauty, as demonstrated by the many precious stones, in contrast to the chaos and ugliness of life depicted outside. The presence of God and absence of evil mean that a temple is not needed. Those in the 'Lamb's book of life' (v.27), ie believers in Jesus, are welcome. The wicked exclude themselves by their behaviour.

Added to this scene, in chapter 22 is a tree-lined river that runs through the city, reminiscent of Ezekiel 47:1–12 and Zechariah 14:8–11 that describe prophetic pictures of waters of life streaming from Jerusalem. There are also hints of Eden, where a river flows out of the garden (see Genesis 2:10).

There is a distinct change in pace from 22:6 as the book of Revelation comes to its conclusion. Verse 11 is not commanding wrongdoers to continue in evil, this is a prophetic declaration of what will continue to take place. Similarly we are reminded of the contrast of those inside and outside the city.

The last verses remind us that respect for God's Word in this book is important. God has not revealed His Word for us to tamper with it, and though these words refer just to Revelation, they can be legitimately used for all of the sixty-six books – each one is an equally precious part of God's revelation to us. Together they point to the centrality of Jesus as the One who brings in all that God intends for the restoration of the world.

When we visit a new city on holiday, my wife and I enjoy taking a bus tour to get an overview of the city and suggestions for places we may want to explore further during our stay. I hope this quick Bible bus tour has intrigued you sufficiently so that you will want to visit or re-visit sections and books of the Bible. Maybe Day 61 will see you returning to a portion of Scripture that especially struck you in the last 60 days.

Why not make regular reading of Scripture a habit, if you don't already do so? As you journey through Scripture you will need a guide and you may want to use a Bible study aid such as those provided by the *Cover to Cover Complete* series at CWR.

My prayer is that your appreciation of God will grow as you continue to encounter Him through the books He has inspired, and that you will learn how your story can be joined with what He is doing. May God bless you richly.

QUESTION TO PONDER

How does this vision of the future help you get today into perspective?

Bibliography

If you are interested in books that also give an overview of the Bible, here are some you may find helpful:

Bartholomew, Craig and Goheen, Michael W., *The Drama of Scripture: Finding Our Place in the Biblical Story* (London: SPCK, 2006)

Goheen, Michael W., *A Light to the Nations: The Missional Church and the Biblical Story* (Grand Rapids, MI: Baker Academic, 2011)

Goldsworthy, Graeme, *Gospel and Kingdom: A Christian Interpretation of the Old Testament* (Milton Keynes: Paternoster Press, 1994)

Greenslade, Philip, *A Passion for God's Story: Discovering Your Place in God's Strategic Plan* (Milton Keynes: Paternoster Press, 2002)

Wright, Chris, *The Mission of God: Unlocking the Bible's Grand Narrative* (Nottingham: IVP, 2006)

National Distributors

UK: (and countries not listed below)

CWR, Waverley Abbey House, Waverley Lane, Farnham, Surrey GU9 8EP.
Tel: (01252) 784700 Outside UK (44) 1252 784700 Email: mail@cwr.org.uk

AUSTRALIA: KI Entertainment, Unit 21 317-321 Woodpark Road, Smithfield, New South Wales 2164.
Tel: 1 800 850 777 Fax: 02 9604 3699 Email: sales@kientertainment.com.au

CANADA: David C Cook Distribution Canada, PO Box 98, 55 Woodslee Avenue, Paris, Ontario N3L 3E5.
Tel: 1800 263 2664 Email: joy.kearley@davidccook.ca

GHANA: Challenge Enterprises of Ghana, PO Box 5723, Accra.
Tel: (021) 222437/223249 Fax: (021) 226227 Email: ceg@africaonline.com.gh

HONG KONG: Cross Communications Ltd, 1/F, 562A Nathan Road, Kowloon.
Tel: 2780 1188 Fax: 2770 6229 Email: cross@crosshk.com

INDIA: Crystal Communications, 10-3-18/4/1, East Marredpalli, Secunderabad – 500026, Andhra Pradesh.
Tel/Fax: (040) 27737145 Email: crystal_edwj@rediffmail.com

KENYA: Keswick Books and Gifts Ltd, PO Box 10242-00400, Nairobi.
Tel: (020) 2226047/312639 Email: sales.keswick@africaonline.co.ke

MALAYSIA: Canaanland Distributors Sdn Bhd, No. 25 Jalan PJU 1A/41B, NZX Commercial Centre, Ara Jaya, 47301 Petaling Jaya, Selangor.
Tel: (03) 7885 0540/1/2 Fax: (03) 7885 0545 Email: info@canaanland.com.my

Salvation Publishing & Distribution Sdn Bhd, 23 Jalan SS 2/64, 47300 Petaling Jaya, Selangor.
Tel: (03) 78766411/78766797 Fax: (03) 78757066/78756360
Email: info@salvationbookcentre.com

NEW ZEALAND: KI Entertainment, Unit 21 317-321 Woodpark Road, Smithfield, New South Wales 2164, Australia.
Tel: 0 800 850 777 Fax: +612 9604 3699 Email: sales@kientertainment.com.au

NIGERIA: FBFM, Helen Baugh House, 96 St Finbarr's College Road, Akoka, Lagos.
Tel: (01) 7747429/4700218/825775/827264 Email: fbfm_1@yahoo.com

PHILIPPINES: OMF Literature Inc, 776 Boni Avenue, Mandaluyong City.
Tel: (02) 531 2183 Fax: (02) 531 1960 Email: gloadlaon@omflit.com

SINGAPORE: Alby Commercial Enterprises Pte Ltd, 95 Kallang Avenue #04-00, AIS Industrial Building, 339420.
Tel: (65) 629 27238 Fax: (65) 629 27235 Email: marketing@alby.com.sg

SRI LANKA: Christombu Publications (Pvt) Ltd, Bartleet House, 65 Braybrooke Place, Colombo 2.
Tel: (9411) 2421073/2447665 Email: christombupublications@gmail.com

USA: David C Cook Distribution Canada, PO Box 98, 55 Woodslee Avenue, Paris, Ontario N3L 3E5, Canada.
Tel: 1800 263 2664 Email: joy.kearley@davidccook.ca

CWR is a Registered Charity – Number 294387
CWR is a Limited Company registered in England – Registration Number 1990308

Know God better and be strengthened spiritually

Our compact, daily Bible-reading notes for adults are published bimonthly and offer a focus for every need. They are available as individual issues or annual subscriptions, in print, in ebook format or by email.

Every Day with Jesus

With around half a million readers, this insightful devotional by Selwyn Hughes is one of the most popular daily Bible-reading tools in the world. A large-print edition is also available.

72-page booklets, 120x170mm

Inspiring Women Every Day

Written by women, for women to inspire, encourage and strengthen.

64-page booklets, 120x170mm

Life Every Day

Apply the Bible to life each day with these challenging life-application notes written by international speaker and well-known author Jeff Lucas.

64-page booklets, 120x170mm

Cover to Cover Every Day

Study one Old Testament and one New Testament book in depth with each issue, and a psalm every weekend. Two well-known Bible scholars each contribute a month's series of daily Bible studies. Covers every book of the Bible in five years.

64-page booklets, 120x170mm

For current prices, subscription options or to order visit www.cwr.org.uk/store
Available online or from Christian bookshops.

Cover to Cover Complete – NIV Edition

Read through the Bible chronologically

Take an exciting, year-long journey through the Bible, following events as they happened.

- See God's strategic plan of redemption unfold across the centuries
- Increase your confidence in the Bible as God's inspired message
- Come to know your heavenly Father in a deeper way

The full text of the flowing NIV provides an exhilarating reading experience and is augmented by our beautiful:

- Illustrations
- Maps
- Charts
- Diagrams
- Timeline

And key Scripture verses and devotional thoughts make each day's reading more meaningful.

ISBN: 978-1-85345-804-0

For current price or to order visit www.cwr.org.uk/store
Available online or from Christian bookshops.

Transforming lives

CWR's vision is to enable people to experience personal transformation through applying God's Word to their lives and relationships.

Our Bible-based training and resources help people around the world to:

- Grow in their walk with God
- Understand and apply Scripture to their lives
- Resource themselves and their church
- Develop pastoral care and counselling skills
- Train for leadership
- Strengthen relationships, marriage and family life

and much more.

Our insightful writers provide daily Bible-reading notes and other resources for all ages, and our experienced course designers and presenters have gained an international reputation for excellence and effectiveness.

CWR's Training and Conference Centres in Surrey and East Sussex, England, provide excellent facilities in idyllic settings - ideal for both learning and spiritual refreshment.

CWR **Applying God's Word** *to everyday life and relationships*

CWR, Waverley Abbey House,
Waverley Lane, Farnham,
Surrey GU9 8EP, UK

Telephone: **+44 (0)1252 784700**
Email: **info@cwr.org.uk**
Website: **www.cwr.org.uk**

Registered Charity No 294387
Company Registration No 1990308